Contemplative Healing

Contemplative Healing

THE CONGREGATION AS HEALING COMMUNITY

Francis Geddes

Foreword by Marcus J. Borg

Afterword by Larry Dossey, MD

iUniverse, Inc.
Bloomington

iUniverse books may be ordered through booksellers or by contacting:

iUniverse
1663 Liberty Drive
Bloomington, IN 47403
www.iuniverse.com
1-800-Authors (1-800-288-4677)

ISBN: 978-1-4502-8344-1 (sc)
ISBN: 978-1-4502-8345-8 (ebook)

Printed in the United States of America

iUniverse rev. date: 2/1/2011

For Virginia

whose steadfast loving support
and editorial eye contributed so much

For Ann

whose commitment to healing is ultimate

CONTENTS

FOREWORD

MARCUS J. BORG

Francis Geddes, as you will learn in this book, is a Christian trainer of healers. His vocation for several decades has been bringing the practice of healing into local congregations, both for the sake of healing and for the sake of revitalizing congregational life.

Francis combines passions not commonly brought together in one person. A pastor and theological progressive with a strong intellectual interest, he is also deeply committed to social justice. Indeed, he has been in jail twice for his involvement in nonviolent protests led by Martin Luther King Jr. and Cesar Chavez. And, most germane to this book, prayer and healing prayer have been at the center of his life and work as a pastor, teacher, and practitioner.

For more than one reason, I am pleased to write a foreword to this book. Its treatment of healing as a spiritual and Christian practice is important for Christians and the church in our time. It creates a framework for seeing healing within the practice of Jesus and early Christianity, attends to the relationship between healing and contemporary medical science, and describes how to introduce the practice of healing into local congregations.

Moreover, it is based upon experience—namely, Francis's experience of training healers in the context of Christian community and his seasoned reflections about that experience. The book thus makes an important and persuasive case for recovering this ancient Christian practice, even as it provides practical suggestions for how to do so.

The second reason is more personal. I have known Francis for almost twenty years. Jesus and the topic of healing brought us together in the summer of 1990. He had read my book *Jesus: A New Vision*, which had been published a couple of years earlier. Two features of that book attracted his attention.

First, I devoted a chapter to the sharp differences between the premodern worldview found in the Bible and the modern Western worldview. The former is a spiritual worldview: it affirms a nonmaterial layer or dimension of reality charged with energy and power. The latter is a materialistic worldview: it presumes that the only "real" world is the space-time world of matter and energy. Within the premodern worldview, paranormal healings are accepted as something that happens. Within the modern worldview, they are not regarded as possible, unless a psychosomatic explanation can be offered. That chapter sharply critiqued the modern worldview with its dogmatic understanding of what is possible and not possible.

Second, I devoted a chapter to Jesus as a healer and exorcist. Within a fuller profile of Jesus as a Jewish mystic, wisdom teacher, and prophet of the Kingdom of God, I affirmed that healing was central to his activity. More healing stories are told about Jesus than about any other figure in the Jewish tradition.

Like Francis, I do not see every healing story in the Gospels as a historically factual account of a specific event, but the overall impression that Jesus was a healer is firmly grounded in his followers' memories of him. Moreover, the Gospels report that his healing activity was largely responsible for his beginning to attract crowds who would listen to his message about the Kingdom of God. He must have been a remarkable healer.

Attracted by the book, Francis took a course from me at Pacific School of Religion in Berkeley, California, where I was a visiting professor. Then he invited me to lead a weeklong retreat sponsored by the Pacific Center for Spiritual Formation, the first of several retreats on which we cooperated in the 1990s. Over the years, we have become friends as well as colleagues. I value him greatly, not only as a friend but also for his wisdom, compassion, and goodness. We can learn much from him.

In this book, Francis provides a way of thinking about healing and prayer that affirms mystery but not magic. The magical way of thinking about God and healing imagines that God answers some prayers but not others, or that God sometimes intervenes but other times does not. Francis rejects the notion of divine intervention as an explanation for paranormal healing, as do I. For both of us, the notion of divine intervention has an enormous theological problem: if one thinks that God sometimes intervenes, how does one account for all the noninterventions?

Yet we are both persuaded that prayer is sometimes a factor in bringing about healing. How to explain this, we do not know. Just as we reject divine intervention as the explanation, we also reject simplistic psychosomatic explanations. Healing prayer has effects, we are convinced, and we prefer to speak of mystery rather than seeking to explain how it is possible. One can affirm healing without knowing the explanatory mechanism.

What makes this book especially valuable is its practical emphasis. Francis describes how to begin a healing ministry in local congregations and describes in detail the healing workshops in which he, and now his daughter, Ann, as well, train people to be healers. Moreover, he expands the notion of healing beyond the curing of physical infirmities to psychological and social healing.

Healing is a comprehensive metaphor within Christianity. Indeed, it is one of the meanings of *salvation,* as suggested by the Latin root of the word. Salvation and salve (a healing substance) come from the same word. *Salvation* means to become whole, to be healed. God's passion, we are both convinced, is to heal a broken world. Christians and others are called to participate in God's passion for mending the world.

ACKNOWLEDGMENTS

I stand on the shoulders of many who have contributed to the content and spirit of this book. Standing there, I am able to see a greater distance and experience a greater depth of insight and wisdom. It is with a sense of deep gratitude that I lift up research psychologist Lawrence LeShan, a man of profound spiritual depth, who was my mentor in healing. I learned from him that healing can be taught and that every one of us is a latent healer, but we just are unaware of this fact.

I am particularly grateful to New Testament scholar Marcus J. Borg, who has taught me a great deal about the historical Jesus and his practice of healing. Dr. Borg has helped me, and thousands of other people, to meet Jesus again for the first time. He has become a good friend and has made many helpful suggestions about organizing the material in the manuscript. He has provided a generous foreword for the book.

I have been moved by the spiritual depth and helpful wisdom of Larry Dossey, MD, who has done more to build a bridge between scientific medicine and the spiritual practice of healing than anyone else in the field. Though trained in scientific medicine, Dossey has the insights of a theologian who has studied the subtleties of intercessory prayer as a healing modality. He has written a gracious afterword, and he helped me to find a wonderful agent.

My devoted wife, Virginia, has spent hundreds of hours over a period of years editing drafts of the manuscript, turning bumpy sentences into smooth prose. Her encouragement, love, and wisdom have made an enormous contribution to my efforts, to the end that the manuscript has finally become a book.

I am indebted to my daughter, Ann, who has been co-leading the healing training with me since 2001. Chapter 2, written by Ann, describes how we teach contemplative healing. She brings a level of spiritual wisdom and sensitivity to others that enables them to recognize their own gifts and to become aware of what is blocking them. A Catholic convert, her early spiritual formation in nondualistic Eastern practices of Buddhist meditation, with Buddhist and Hindu teachers of body prayer, yoga, and music leadership, have made a significant contribution to the contemplative healing training that we do together.

My profound gratitude goes to Melissa Horton, who urged me some years ago to set up advanced training workshops for those who wanted to learn how to teach this process under supervision. Today there are more than a dozen individuals who teach this form of contemplative healing.

The Reverend Canon Marianne Wells Borg of Trinity Episcopal Cathedral in Portland, Oregon, has created an effective ministry of healing there with strong lay leadership based on the healing training that I have conducted for the Trinity people over many years. Canon Borg has combined the contemplative music of Taizé with healing prayer and laying on of hands in a monthly Sunday evening service that draws many people from miles around. She has introduced healing in the chapel after people have received the Eucharist in the Sunday services. There are at least a dozen services of healing in Oregon congregations, representing various denominations, that are modeled upon her Taizé healing service. For her ability to fashion a healing ministry and translate insights from the healing training into a contemplative service of chanting and healing, I am deeply grateful.

The healing teams and clergy in congregations where I have interviewed, named below, have made a significant contribution to understanding the development and practice of healing in the life of mainline congregations. I have learned from them new ways that the Spirit unfolds in the life of the spiritual community that Jesus founded: Westminster Presbyterian Church, Portland, Oregon, the Reverend Jim Moiso, then pastor, and the late Judy Sprunger, healing team; St. Aidan's Episcopal Church, San Francisco, the Right Reverend Bavi Rivera, then rector, and Patricia Brown, healing team; Peace Lutheran Church, Danville, California, the Reverend Steve Harms, pastor, and Chris Huntze, healing team; Unity in the Valley, Eugene, Oregon, the Reverend Baine Palmer, then minister; Unity in Roseburg, Oregon, the Reverend Inge Tarantola, then minister; Unity in Ashland, Oregon, and the Reverend Sherry Lady, then minister.

The witness of healing team members and clergy provide a model of the practice of compassion in the life of a congregation. It is clear to me that the Spirit is profoundly at work in these congregations and their clergy.

My deepest appreciation and thanks to the Reverend Patricia Moore and the Reverend Matthew Lawrence of the Episcopal Church of the Incarnation in Santa Rosa, California. They enabled and supported the establishment of an effective healing ministry. I am part of the healing team there and helped in its development and practice.

Profound thanks and deep gratitude go to my agent, Barbara Deal, who guided me in many helpful ways, especially when dealing with publishers. My spiritual director, the Reverend Zoila Schoenbrun, provided wisdom, spiritual clarity, and insight through the years of preparation. Her encouragement and support meant so much to me.

I am grateful to Dr. Sandra Brown, retired director of the Lloyd Pastoral Counseling Center at the San Francisco Theological Seminary in San Anselmo, California. When I was a spiritual director on her staff, she read my manuscript with the eyes of a scholar and improved the result.

The Reverend Brian Cochran, one of my students, who teaches contemplative healing, spent many long hours editing and reformatting a number of chapters to meet the publisher's specifications. He made a real contribution to achieving an earlier publication date. Heartfelt gratitude to Elianne Obadia, The Writer's Midwife, for her skillful editing of chapters 3 and 7.

Profound thanks go to my nephew Jim Geddes, whose support and prayers were helpful during the difficult times of waiting for the next step.

To all of the above I offer my appreciation and gratitude for the encouragement, support, and compassion extended to me during those years of writing.

INTRODUCTION

All healing begins with pain. Every person alive has the capacity to pass on a healing force/energy to someone who is in pain. This is a book about practicing compassion within a spiritual community. Offering healing prayer with others can be a part of one's spiritual path. However, that individual journey is deepened when God's compassionate gift of healing occurs within a congregation. Every great religion in the world has a tradition of healing wherein this ability is practiced, accepted, and acknowledged. In the Christian tradition, healing is not something that a person does; rather, one participates in God's grace. God and Christ are the healers.

Contemplative healing is grounded in the spiritual practices of contemplative prayer. These practices enable the healer to be more compassionate, totally present in prayer with the person in pain, intensely focused, and not distracted. The person praying needs to learn how to get out of the way so that this divine healing force/energy can enter into the relationship of prayer between the healer, the person in pain, and God.

I observed this healing process practiced in the life of twenty congregations on the West Coast in mostly mainline Protestant denominations. Contemplative healing is a way of being deeply present to God and compassionately present to the person who receives healing.

Jesus introduced healing into the Judaism of his day as an essential spiritual practice of his teaching. He saw healing as evidence that the Kingdom of God is at hand, here and now. He insisted that this reign of God is present in our midst but that we do not have eyes to see what is in front of us. Doubtless Jesus taught his disciples to heal, and he expected them to offer healing when he sent them out to proclaim the reign of God. New Testament scholar John Dominic Crossan suggests that Jesus healed several peasant fishermen in Galilee who later became disciples and went on to heal others.

Chapter 2 describes how we teach a contemplative healing process. We learn how to let go so that the healing force/energy or Spirit can enter the relationship of healer/healee to do the actual healing. Taking this practice into a congregation can benefit the entire community as a more compassionate and spiritually nurtured focus grows.

During the church's first three hundred years, healing was a very important spiritual practice. In the United States today, healing is acknowledged but not seriously practiced in most mainline Protestant congregations. This book lifts up the stories of five congregations, their laity and clergy, where healing is practiced and taken seriously.

Individual lay people and clergy who practice healing prayer regularly often notice a gentle inward transformation in themselves and discover a deeper identity. Recorded here are a number of stories of individuals who receive healing prayer and were opened into a loving Source wherein they experienced transformation. Not only do they know that they are cared for and loved, but they experience it firsthand in the prayers and laying on of hands. Every time a healing prayer is offered, some of the healing force/energy rubs off on the healer as it passes through to the person who is ill.

Scientific studies in mind/body medicine over the past forty years confirm what many in the church knew in the early centuries: prayer for healing works. It is somewhat surprising that today some medical researchers seem more interested in how healing prayer works than theologians and leaders in the church. One purpose of this book is to help build a bridge across the gulf that has separated science and religion for more than three hundred years.

A number of nurses and doctors who practice in the emerging field of Complementary Medicine, Alternative Medicine, or Integral Medicine point out that there is a difference between healing and curing. The goal of healing is to enable an ill person to become whole, whereas curing focuses on recovery from illness and the alleviation of symptoms. A person slowly dying may have a courageous attitude toward their situation and demonstrate a beautiful inner wholeness. Such an individual is not cured, but dies a whole person who is, in that sense, "healed." This is a helpful distinction between healing and curing. (See further discussion of this issue in chapter 3 on Paul's experience and in chapter 8.) Sometimes prayers are not answered in the way they are asked, and that is part of the mystery of God's grace.

In a larger context, healing takes different forms. In one form, it can lift the burden of pain from an individual who is ill, as reported in these pages. In another form, this same loving force/energy of God can help to heal a sick society that is suffering from racism. In the 1950s and 1960s, Martin Luther King Jr. functioned as a healer for a sick society. The loving force/energy of God is the same whether healing a sick individual or a sick society; it just manifests in a different form. Love is the bottom line in both kinds of healing,

This book describes how the loving spirit of God and Christ function in a community, by alleviating pain and bringing wholeness. The ministry of healing can help any congregation become a more compassionate community. Interviews with individuals and stories of transformation in this book describe how compassion is empowered by prayer and how healing is enabled by the grace of God. Any individual or congregation can learn to cooperate with grace by learning to offer healing prayer as a spiritual discipline. The healing itself is in God's hands.

CHAPTER 1

On Being Drawn to Healing

Although we seem to be different individuals inhabiting separate bodies, we are intimately connected with each other at some level of the mind. This image has surfaced consistently throughout human history. It permeates the language of poets, artists, and mystics, and has been repeatedly understood by spiritual adepts in all the great religious traditions.[1]

—LARRY DOSSEY, MD

There was pain when I moved my thumb. I sat there in a circle of a dozen people who offered prayer for my healing. Ten minutes later there was no pain whatsoever. I was dumbfounded, surprised, and amazed. That was the first time that the personal reality of healing bore in upon me. It was on a Sunday evening in 1972, and happened during a meeting of the Spiritual Frontiers Fellowship when I was minister of the First Congregational Church in San Rafael, California. In an evening series, we had been studying mystical prayer and life after death, and that particular night the subject was healing. The resource person leading the class had some experience in healing. He was about to do a demonstration and asked if anyone in the room was in pain at that particular time. Those of us gathered were silent. No one said a word for an entire minute, and then I hesitantly raised my hand, saying, "It is a very insignificant pain, but I sprained my thumb this afternoon in the yard pulling Scotch broom." The leader seemed to give a sigh of relief because he finally had a subject for his demonstration.

We were from many different backgrounds: some were church members, whereas others were spiritual seekers who were not part of the church. He asked people to be in silent prayer together for the healing of my thumb, each praying in his or her own way. For some it was silent verbal prayer, for others it was visualization prayer—seeing light around my hand—and for still others it was silent meditation for healing. Some asked for Jesus's presence.

I had believed that prayer for healing could be effective, but it had never happened to me. Nothing that I studied in theological seminary had prepared me for such an experience. During the weeks and months following, I read everything I could find about healing prayer and healing in the New Testament. My pursuit of the subject included going to lectures, talking to people who practiced healing, and attending the annual conference of the Spiritual Frontiers Fellowship in Chicago. That release of pain rattled my belief system and propelled me to pursue the mystery of healing into a deeper level.

Since then, the study and practice of healing has been a significant part of my spiritual journey for more than thirty years. Healing prayer and laying on of hands are particular spiritual practices that Jesus inaugurated long ago. It is part of our life in God for those of us who follow it. My spiritual director, the Reverend Zoila Schoenbrun, suggests, "Through the practice of healing, Jesus tells us who God is and what God can do through us." It seems to me that any healing we receive is a manifestation, evidence of the "Good News" of God that Jesus proclaimed.

Looking back over the years, it occurs to me that in one sense healing has been part of my life from the very beginning. My mother was a physician. I grew up in a home where healing was in the air we breathed. I literally drank in healing with my mother's milk. She recounted coming home to nurse me after administering chloroform anesthetic to a patient. My father noticed that on days when she had administered chloroform, I would go to sleep in a few minutes after beginning to nurse. He figured out that I was not sleeping, but was being anesthetized because of the fumes still in her clothing. After that, she changed clothes before nursing me on the days that she had given chloroform. I no longer fell asleep at her breast while nursing. I absorbed a healing atmosphere from my earliest days with my mother's milk.

She brought a high level of commitment to patients in her medical practice, and later as school physician for Orange County Schools in California, during the 1930s and '40s. She did not formally teach her children about commitment to serving others in need. However, she modeled it and lived it out in her daily life.

Growing up in Orange County, California, my two brothers and I did not attend church. My mother had attended a fundamentalist boarding school in Massachusetts during the earliest years of the twentieth century. Fire and brimstone were preached in required chapel services. She had a deep, powerful belief in God but rejected the church as rigid and judgmental. In high school, I believed that it was impossible to be a Christian and have intellectual integrity at the same time.

During my first year in the army during World War II, I discovered that most of my friends attended chapel or went to church in towns near the base. I went with them because they were my friends, and I liked to sing the gospel songs. Then in 1943, the scales fell from my eyes when I read a book by Harry Emerson Fosdick, *On Becoming a Real Person*. He was a national figure and minister of Riverside Church in New York. I discovered, much to my surprise, that it was indeed possible to have intellectual integrity and be a Christian at the same time. I wrote Dr. Fosdick a letter of appreciation and gratitude for the book some years later, just before going to Yale Divinity School. He wrote a warm response that included, "To have helped one man like yourself would have made it worthwhile writing the book… It is very gratifying to know that I have been of assistance to you in finding your way into a satisfying faith and a clear sense of vocation. I lift a prayer for you now that the years ahead may be rich with an ever deepening conviction about

God and an ever increasing happiness in your work." (personal communication, 1949).

During 1944, I went to a Congregational church in Honolulu every other Sunday for more than a year, from my air base in Kahuku, Oahu. In the sermons, I was given an intellectual framework that grounded my faith. It was a huge shift. The war ended while I was aboard a troopship bound for Okinawa. We disembarked on the island in September 1945, where I served a bleak four months on the island. Those were some of the worst months of my life. There were not enough ships to bring the 100,000 troops home. We felt abandoned as we sat there, month after month. The despair was so deep that in October and November there was an average of one suicide a week. All of us were suffering from depression. I have never prayed more fervently in my life, or come as close to falling apart emotionally. I survived and felt that God had been with me in those terrible depths. Returning to the States from Okinawa in January 1946, I wanted to finish my undergraduate work and then go to law school. I hoped to heal people's pain and suffering from injustice. I wanted to serve. I longed to become another "Clarence Darrow for the Defense." Stanford Law School was my ultimate goal, so I transferred to Stanford from UCLA as a junior in spring quarter of 1947, hoping that would pave my way toward entering law school there.

MEETING HARRY AND EMILIA RATHBUN

During the summer quarter of 1947, I attended weekly evening discussions on the teachings of Jesus held in the Palo Alto home of Professor Harry Rathbun and his wife, Emilia. They invited students into their home to discuss the teachings of Jesus articulated by the New Testament scholar Henry Burton Sharman. They had studied the records of Jesus during summers with Sharman, camping out in the Canadian woods. Sharman saw Jesus primarily as a teacher of wisdom, and the Rathbuns presented him as a kind of Jewish Socrates. Harry and Emilia were a very dynamic duo. They made Jesus come alive in a way that was quite new for me. When the summer quarter was over, I decided to continue my studies in Jesus's teachings with the Rathbuns for three weeks during vacation. They called their study "Sequoia Seminar." It was held at Asilomar, a conference ground on the ocean near Monterey, California.

During that retreat, I had a surprising conversion experience that radically changed the direction of my life. One morning, during the first session, Emilia put a challenge to the group. "If you think that you can direct your life more effectively than God can, then go right ahead by yourself. But if you think God can do a better job directing and guiding your life than you can, then turn it over to God." I had plenty of evidence that directing my own life was not working well; things were sometimes chaotic. Standing under a pine tree during the break, I said to God, "Things have been going badly for me. My girlfriend has tossed me over. I feel like I'm at sea, and I'm ready to turn the whole mess over to you! Take it." I returned to the second part of the morning session and thought no more about it.

In the middle of the second session, Harry Rathbun was describing the way that we find ourselves cut off from God. He told us that it was like living inside a hard shell that surrounds us completely. The light of God is outside of the shell, always in every moment seeking to get in but unable to find an opening to enter. Then something traumatic happens in our life that strikes a heavy blow to the shell. It cracks, and the light of God moves through the crack and touches the tender center of the heart. As I sat there, listening intently, I suddenly became aware that I was in two places at once. I was in the room, but at the same time I was also in outer space, billions of miles away. I heard three beautiful soprano voices singing without words and interweaving magnificent melodies. I was stunned with joy. Waves of profound beauty washed through me. I could hear people in the room speaking softly, but the singing was much louder. That shift in consciousness lasted about forty-five seconds or a minute. Then, suddenly, I was no longer in two places at the same time, but back in the room, and the singing stopped. I sat there amazed and grateful for the intense beauty that had moved me so deeply. It was overwhelming.

After a few minutes, I began to think about what had happened. The thought came to me, *I just heard voices. Did I experience a psychotic episode?* I was a little worried, and I talked to a fellow participant, Ray Magee, sharing my experience and question. He said, "You have not had a psychotic episode. You have just had a classic conversion experience. Read William James's *The Varieties of Religious Experience*, and you will discover that many other people have had very similar experiences."

Later I read James with much anticipation and discovered that for hundreds of years many people in various parts of the world have heard the voice of the Holy, similar to my experience, and others have had visions with or without an auditory component. James said that our culture had no way to understand or process this kind of spiritual/visionary experience and, therefore, labeled it mental illness.

MEETING HOWARD THURMAN

I was radically changed as I began to pursue my spiritual development, based on this opening experience. Within a year, I had dropped my plans to enter law school and decided to enter a theological seminary. The next year, I met Howard Thurman, who spoke at a student YMCA–YWCA conference at Asilomar during Christmas vacation of 1948. He was an educated mystic and minister of The Church for the Fellowship of All Peoples in San Francisco, which was 50 percent African-American, 45 percent white, and about 5 percent Asian in its makeup. Dr. Thurman was an African-American. Early in 1949, I drove to San Francisco to ask him if I could volunteer as an intern during the summer of 1949, before entering Yale Divinity School that fall. He welcomed me. Over the years, he became my spiritual mentor. He influenced my life in God in a deep and profound way that has stayed with me to this day. For him, Jesus was a mystic, a prophet, and a spiritual companion. Thurman's prayers were a bridge into the Holy. One felt more whole as a result of participating in the worship.

After I graduated from Yale Divinity School in 1952, Dr. Thurman invited me to become his Assistant Minister at Fellowship Church. Several years later, Dr. Thurman was called to become Dean of Chapel at Boston University. I became minister of the church in 1955.

MEETING MARTIN LUTHER KING JR.

In the summer of 1961, I was invited to attend a one-day conference of religious leaders who gathered from various parts of the country in Jackson, Mississippi, to hear Dr. Martin Luther King Jr. I met Dr. King the morning of July 21, over a cup of coffee in the dining room of Tougaloo Christian College. Later in the morning, he urged us to visit local leaders to attempt to bring about reconciliation and healing to the painful illness of racism. Those visits were fruitless. In the late afternoon, Dr. King suggested that we divide in two groups: one group would join with CORE, and in effect becoming Freedom Riders, testing the segregated dining facilities at the Jackson Airport; the second group would fly to Washington to meet with Attorney General Robert Kennedy. That afternoon I volunteered to join the group going to the airport, and were arrested for breach of peace. Each of us was fined $200 and given a four-month jail sentence by the Jackson Municipal Court. I went to jail as a Freedom Rider with eight others who attended the conference.[2] The next morning the group was out on bail, and that afternoon I flew back to San Francisco to await my return to Jackson for trial. The other group flew to Washington to meet with Attorney General Robert Kennedy. None of the nine jailed had to serve the four-month jail term because our convictions were overturned on appeal.

In the 1960s, healing the painful wound of racism took many forms, including nonviolent resistance and civil disobedience. For me, that experience was a spiritual turning point. Inspired by Jesus, Dr. King was a healer who sought to bring justice through nonviolent resistance to the pain-wracked conflicts of racism in a sick society.

MEETING LAWRENCE LESHAN

In the spiritual tradition of India, there is an oft-quoted saying, "When the student is ready, the teacher will appear." After the healing of my painful thumb, I began looking high and low for someone who could teach me healing. I had heard the research psychologist Lawrence LeShan speak on healing at a Spiritual Frontiers Fellowship Conference in Chicago in 1972. The following year I phoned him in New York to invite him to speak at a Spiritual Frontiers event in Oakland, California, that fall. His calendar was full, but he asked me if I would like to attend his five-day residential healing training near Santa Cruz, California, in March 1974. I was ready and said that I would. "When the student is ready the teacher will appear" happened to me in meeting Lawrence LeShan.

Two weeks before the healing training was to begin I had a dream. I was in a cabin with about ten other people who were seated in a circle. The disquieting thing about the dream was that I was standing on my head! On the first day of the healing training, I was astonished because it was held inside the large cabin that I had seen in my dream. Looking back, those five days learning healing from LeShan had certainly turned my life upside down. LeShan some months later asked me to become a member of his healing research project.

Dr. LeShan agreed to offer advice for my Doctor of Ministry dissertation that I was writing at the San Francisco Theological Seminary in San Anselmo, California. My Dissertation Project included training four congregations on the West Coast in the LeShan healing method that I had set into a Christian context. It was titled "Healing Training in the Church." He also helped me to secure a foundation grant to conduct the dissertation research. I wanted the dissertation to become an entrée for healing ministry into mainstream Protestant congregations. Meeting Lawrence LeShan changed the focus of my ministry and professional life. He was convinced that every person had the innate capacity to offer healing to others. Training and practice was all that was needed. I was powerfully drawn to healing training and practice as I continued my pastoral ministry.

In writing my dissertation, I found it difficult to explore the field of sacramental healing empirically because the scientific method and the theological method covered only a certain portion of the ground that needed to be explored. Healing prayer research lies somewhere in an area "between" science and theology, fact and belief. I found that quantum physics was a helpful discipline in this area of research because it also finds itself in this area of the between, where that which one perceives as fact is significantly influenced and changed by what one observes and believes. In quantum physics, it is called the "observer effect," where just the presence of the observer influences and changes the outcome of the experiment. I began to wonder if healing prayer, in similar fashion, provided a kind of "observer effect" phenomenon that could influence and change the outcome of an illness because of the intentional presence of the person offering prayer. It seemed to me that the "observer effect" in quantum physics was a mechanism similar to the mechanism of healing prayer. In no way does this observation explain the mystery of how healing prayer operates, but I found that it provided an interesting parallel.

In my dissertation, I concluded that Jesus commissioned his followers to offer healing as part of their proclamation of the Good News. Their ministry in the first century was modeled on Jesus's own style of ministry. People in the church today need to be exposed to a kind of healing theory and practice that lifts up the biblical witness and at the same time does not ignore the culture's scientific worldview. Writing the dissertation gave me a stronger biblical, historical, scientific, and theological foundation for my work in teaching healing within mainstream Protestantism.

MEETING TILDEN EDWARDS AND GERALD MAY

In 1983–1984, I underwent training as a spiritual director at the Shalem Institute for Spiritual Formation in Washington, D.C. Upon completing the training, it became clear to me that the healing retreat, with its heavy emphasis on spiritual practices and prayer, was a particular style of spiritual formation.

I had been practicing contemplative prayer on a daily basis since my junior year in college, but Tilden Edwards and Gerald May at Shalem introduced me to the importance of spiritual direction and gave me a framework for my spiritual practice that was grounded in psychological insight and the tradition of Christian contemplative prayer. This was another turning point for me. I stand on the shoulders of all my teachers and mentors over the years. I am deeply indebted to them for what I have learned along the way in pursuing my spiritual journey.

HEALING TRAINING IN THE CHURCH

Since 1976, I have trained about nine hundred individuals, a dozen people at a time, in these five-day training retreats. Since 2001, my daughter, Ann, has co-led these retreats with me and enriched them by adding yoga, music, and her spiritual sensitivity to the process. She has deepened and improved the training in many ways.

Over the years, I have consulted with about twenty congregations in the development of their ministries of healing. Teaching healing is the most rewarding work I have ever done in my life. Students learn a practice that I call Contemplative Healing. Because this healing training is grounded in daily, contemplative practice, individuals who follow this practice for some time find that their personal centeredness begins to deepen. Slowly, the person begins an inward transformation toward clarity and wholeness. To see the Spirit at work in another person's life is enormously rewarding.

Those of us offering healing prayer often experience gratitude, humility, and awe in our praying as we become instruments in God's hands. We feel that it is a privilege to be a conduit for the work of the Spirit.

BEING DRAWN TO HEALING

There are many things that draw me to healing. During most of my life, being in the presence of pain in one form or another has motivated me to respond. In my later years, that response has been healing prayer for painful illness. Before that, it was being part of the civil rights movement that included civil disobedience in response to the painful sickness of racism. In the presence of God, I do not feel helpless in responding to pain. There is something that I can do. Healing prayer is a particular resource for pastors and others of us who find ourselves confronted by the presence of other people's pain.

In the church, we are called to love, to be and become our brother's keeper. That innate capacity for love and healing resides deeply in every person, inside or outside the church. We are all healers, but we don't know it. God would call it out from the deepest part of our being. That is what Jesus did when he urged and taught his followers to go forth and proclaim the Good News and to heal. In the past thirty years, my way of pursuing that goal has been to teach Christian healing as an integral part of the Good News. These years have been richly rewarding for me in ways that are difficult to describe. I have been touched by an "amazing grace." For me, it all started with the pain of a sprained thumb.

CHAPTER 2

Learning the Healing Practice

by Ann A. Geddes

Our soul is oned to God, unchangeable goodness, and therefore between God and our soul there is neither wrath nor forgiveness because there is no between.[3]

—Julian of Norwich

How does one enter the state of "no between"? We are born into a culture that worships separation, striving, personal effort, winning and losing. How can we as mere humans break free from these bonds of everyday stress and scarring? The answer is, with God's grace, and with practice. We can take ourselves into the place of quiet within so that we can hear the heartbeat of a loving and present Earth, and a loving and present God.

We are not raised to be aware of or to listen to this reality, this Kingdom of God on Earth. And so we look for opportunities to train ourselves, with patience, to find a new radio station on the dial, tuning ourselves until we have a clear connection. This tuning, this listening, is done via the practice of meditation and silence. By gradually dropping the habitual boundaries that separate us from one another, we remember our oneness, our holy state of connection. In this state—connected inside, connected outside—we can be used as instruments, as vessels for the healing grace that comes through us from God.

The Contemplative Healing training is a five-day process in which we experience being connected, joined in this way, enjoying together the delicately interwoven elements of silence, meditation, healing, friendship with each other, and communion with God. Below is a description that can be no more than an indication of how we spend those days, for each group unfolds in its own special way, and the transformation that occurs for each person cannot be put into words.

EMBRACING MEDITATION AND HOLY SILENCE

We begin in a circle, a group of twelve to sixteen individuals who don't know one another or what to expect. We gather and share what brought us to the healing retreat. Together, we then begin a journey of awakening. People come to the healing training for many different reasons. Perhaps a friend or spiritual director has recommended it, or they themselves have felt inspired or led to participate. Or they may have been feeling the beginnings of a quiet awakening and are seeking a place to explore it. Some have been called to healing work and are seeking directed training. Whatever the motivations, we enter together the process of opening our heart to God, and for many it is the first time their heart has ever been deeply awakened.

What causes the heart to be awakened in this context? First and foremost, it is the silence. Many people have never spent time being truly still and quiet. Whether God whispers to you in words, or reveals Himself as the presence of love in you, or makes Himself known in any other way—the practice begins with the connection that happens in deep silence.

The calming of the mind and stilling of the soul begin with some simple ten-minute meditations. The first practices we teach are simple breath awareness exercises: counting our breaths, watching the rise and fall of the breath, or saying the Jesus Prayer.

We listen to the in-breath and the out-breath, giving our mind a point of focus so we can enter into a state of being where we are quiet, connected, and whole, anchored into the Earth and into the heavens. In, out… like waves on the shore calming our nervous insistence that we are in charge, our minds running the show—when in fact it is God who has His hands on the steering wheel.

The breath exercises are followed by a meditation in which we focus on a small object, keeping our eyes open. Traditionally, one gazes at a brass doorknob on a plain black background, a piece of black velvet. We use instead a small paper match. The purpose of the gazing exercise is to develop focus and concentration, to align the mind—which naturally wishes to leap off in every direction—to one point of focus.

This quieting allows us to become aware of the undercurrents of depth that constantly stir our soul, allowing us to deepen into our natural state of connection to God within and to God without in these contemplative prayer exercises.

The meditations then branch into visualization exercises, to train the mind to visualize as well as to become quiet and calm. These are arranged to gradually open us into a deeper and deeper practice; they become more complex, and several meditations are extended in length. As we become more practiced, we include icon gazing and a meditation of connection between two individuals, drawing ourselves ever more deeply into connection and depth.

Included is a grounding practice so that the ethereal can be anchored by Earth and keep everyone focused and present to the present moment. We may also practice walking meditation. To refresh the mind during the training, we also sing, chant, pray, and move our bodies. Yoga or simple stretching movements are used to relax the body and refresh the mind. The purpose of yoga when it was practiced in ancient times was not merely to achieve a fit and healthy body, but to create union between heaven and earth, human beings and God. Bhakti yoga (the yoga of devotion), one of the oldest forms of yoga, encourages love of God and devotion to the grace and presence of God in our lives. So our bodies, too, become instruments of grace in this healing practice.

We meditate and do these contemplative practices over the course of two to three days before we begin the healing practice itself. Gradually, we accelerate our ability to visualize, our ability to silence the mind and to be in the presence of God. Some of these practices are continued throughout the training. They support us to remain open to the influence and direction of God, within our souls and within our group as a whole.

At night we are silent. The burden of conversation is lifted, and we enter the quiet and abandon, temporarily, the need to analyze and understand, to qualify everything. We keep silence through the first exercises of the morning until breakfast. We often find time for humor and laughter at lunch or dinner. We stay in silence after dinner each evening until breakfast the next morning. At mealtimes we laugh, joke, take delight in one another's presence, and occasionally enjoy a meal in silence.

EMBRACING HEALING

We teach that we ourselves do not heal, but that it is God who heals; we are instruments in His hands. And we come from the understanding that anyone can heal, with practice, concentration, and presence.

On the first night, after supper, we hear a lecture on healing, about Jesus calling all his disciples to heal—whether they felt willing, ready, and able, or not. This was the call to share the Kingdom of God with one another and transform suffering in the world. Who are we to be given such gifts? We may wonder, but we are asked only to practice with diligence and patience the exercises that are presented to us, grateful that we have been invited into the pool of God's loving power.

In the healing practice itself, we want to clear ourselves of the everyday internal chatter our minds tend to be filled with. Gradually our attunement becomes increasingly clear, with less and less interference from our living-a-regular-life habit. We practice to become open channels of His love, getting ourselves out of the way—our fears, hopes, egos, dreams. It is as if we were stepping out and standing beside ourselves to let God in, let Christ in.

On the third day, we begin the healing. By that time, we have become entrained into a unity, a wholeness that did not exist before we gathered together and began our practices. We enter into prayer woven together, knit to one another in practice and in purpose. It is from this unity, this joined place, that we heal.

We begin each healing with a breath awareness exercise followed by a visual concentration exercise, so that we may become silent, still, and attuned to God's presence.

One of the leaders begins with a prayer for the one to be healed. The healers gather around in a circle, first praying silently while seated. Toward the close of the healing, we lay hands on the subject. Alternatively, we gather close to the subject and lay on hands or hold our hands above the person. Everyone in the retreat has an opportunity for his or her own healing, whether it be physical, emotional, or spiritual. You can ask for healing in any area of your life that calls to you.

During the healing, we focus our love intently on our fellow subject. We empty ourselves to be channels for God's love and communion. The healing takes place as we abandon our will, our idea of what healing should take place, into the hands of God. We are praying for a person's soul, not the personality, so that if any one of us has the experience of not particularly connecting with the subject, we can pray for his or her inner being with all our heart and all our soul, without the interference of the "little ego."

In this way, we meet God in union with the one being healed and offer that person up. It is this linking up with God that is holy, that is healing. Each one who is being healed takes a journey into the arms of God, carried by their brothers and sisters who are loving them into a pure state of union with the Beloved.

After being healed, you may feel as if you've been bathed in the intense heat of God's warming love. Or you may feel cool and pleasant and calm. You may feel a bit disconnected from the earth, having been sent so deeply into the heavens. Some people take time away and alone to integrate, resting quietly, and some are moved to tears. Someone else may say they feel as though they have been tumbled in the ocean, tossed around and around as the waves pushed them up onto shore. All of us, however, leave human time and enter the time of God for a reawakening to our true nature.

After the healing, as a group we may hold silence, sing softly, or breathe deeply to transition back to our individuated selves. We release the healing space as we trust and honor the unfolding of the healing in the hours, days, and weeks to come. Each healing, then, is an unfolding—not necessarily a sudden marked place in time, but a movement toward wholeness and recovery.

EMBRACING THE COMMUNITY OF SOUL

What happens to us as we practice together so tightly woven in love? We drop our hard shells and can meet in a place of mutuality, not separate and apart as individuals intent on striving, but in a place of shared communion where the force of God is coming through us as a united whole.

This in and of itself is healing—to connect with others deeply on the level of the soul rather than meeting on the surface of the personality and skirting the edges of connection. In this way, we can reach down into the root of ourselves and touch the part of us that is one with God.

The seeds of love and presence that God has planted within us at our birth take root and grow in this environment that nurtures and encourages growing into love, growing into community. Once we have spent five days together healing and practicing, we are connected in ways we cannot completely comprehend. We have practiced loving kindness. We have practiced carrying one another into the arms of God. So we are bound in love in a particular way. Whether we like or dislike each other's personalities, we are bound in love at the soul level. And this is where the healing takes place: deep within. A place so sacred only God knows how to awaken it.

Of course, difficulties may arise on the way. We may become cranky, not accepting, or judgmental of one another. All is not perfect bliss. Charles R. Ringma, author of *The Seeking Heart: A Journey with Henri Nouwen*, quotes Nouwen in describing this tension:

We cannot place our hope in what the other will do for us in friendship and community. We can only hope in the goodness that God gives in the midst of life together. Nouwen came to this during his time at the Abbey of Genesee in upstate New York. He writes, "[A] monastery is not built to solve problems, but to praise the Lord in the midst of them."[4]

But at every point of difficulty, hope dawns as if someone had lit an inner candle, and a burning begins—a burning of hope, faith, and passion. And by that light, we find our way, working together to deliver the word of God that we should love one another here on Earth, perhaps one of the most challenging commandments.

EMBRACING TRANSFORMATION

Without our realizing it, our habits, life experiences, and habitual patterns bind us to a particular way of seeing and experiencing the world. We aim to break this pattern through rigorous practice and training in seeing with the heart. We bring ourselves into a natural way of being, into our birthright, into the blessings that God has for us that may have remained hidden or inaccessible because of the distractions and distresses of everyday life. This training helps us break free from our habitual way of seeing and to practice seeing with the eyes of love, God, acceptance, not the eyes of separation and defeat.

So, too, it is a giving up, a surrender into peace and connection—into a quieter place where the love and presence of God can reign and direct our souls as they are longing to be directed. We are directed into connection with God, into connection and into love with one another.

The Contemplative Healing training is also an awakening. A dawning. A remembering. The soul becomes still and quiet and alive. There is great joy and perhaps tears as the layers of the untrue, unconnected, dead self are peeled away to release the living, deepening, alive, and loving self. It is a sacred practice and one into which we do not enter lightly.

The journey isn't necessarily all peace and tranquility. In our awakening, we may squirm, resist, struggle. But our hearts will call to us constantly until we answer that call. The training, then, is a practice of quieting our busy nature until we can listen fully to the cry of a lonely heart and sense God's response to that cry.

Surely we are born with the seeds of knowing, knowing the depth and breadth of God's love. This training is, at its core, about learning how to remember that perfected state of love.

EMBRACING LOVE, CARRYING IT INTO THE WORLD

Imagine being bathed in a pool of God's loving kindness, being loved in every length and breadth of your soul, your being, in all the places you are known and unknown, hidden and transparent. We are each loved by God, so fiercely and exactly as we are in this moment—not after we've perfected ourselves, become kinder, more full of grace—right now as we are in this very moment in all the ways we stumble, are less than perfect, are rude, cranky, unaware, human. We are loved so fiercely that our smaller selves cannot comprehend or even imagine the depth to which we are loved. Through the practices of this training, we step into and partake of that pool of love, acceptance, and connection and become more and more able to offer that to others.

We are being asked to become instruments of God's peace. And so we follow this instruction as best we can with all our imperfections, uncertainties, and worries—that we are somehow not enough, lacking, or too ordinary to proceed with this type of work. But over and over again, we return to our trust in God and the instruction Christ gave us to go forth into the world and heal. Joy takes up residence within us as we walk more and more in the way of the Spirit. We are directed to our own delight and hope. We can view the world, for a little while at least, with the eyes of God.

CHAPTER 3

Jesus: The Healer Who Taught Healing

We cannot, however, assume that we will receive what our ego self-image might understand as healing. Our egos are very caught up in symptoms of brokenness. God in Christ promises to be about a deeper work of healing in the fundamental sources of brokenness. "I came that they may have life, and have it abundantly" (John 10:10). That life rises from an identity that ultimately flows from the wholeness of God rather than any self-contained source. This identity with God is the fundamental healing.[5]

—Tilden Edwards

In the words of Dietrich Bonhoeffer, "Jesus was the man for others."[6] Nowhere is this caring more evident than in his repeated acts of healing with those burdened by pain and illness. The image of Jesus as a compassionate teacher and gifted healer with great authority steps off the pages of the New Testament into our modern view. Perhaps it is difficult to comprehend this image in the twenty-first century because today healing prayer is not widely recognized as an effective resource for health in technological societies.

On the first day of his public ministry, Jesus is presented by Mark as a powerful healer. Mark recounts the story of the deranged man with an unclean spirit who interrupted Jesus's speaking in the synagogue at Capernaum. Jesus called the unclean spirit to come out of the man, and the man was restored to his true self. "They were all amazed, and they kept asking one another, 'What is this? A new teaching—with authority! He commands even the unclean spirits, and they obey him.' " (Mark 1:27).

For Mark, the new teaching was not only something that Jesus said but what he *did*, the healing itself.[7] Eighteen healing stories appear in the first ten chapters of the book of Mark, and many of these stories were later borrowed by Luke and Matthew. They point to the very prominent role that healing plays in the Gospel records. These stories also deepen our understanding of Jesus's message, showing that God's healing action can come through human instruments used to usher in the Kingdom of God.

What was the source of his remarkable power to heal and cast out demons? The explanation that I find most helpful comes from Jesus scholar Marcus J. Borg, who describes Jesus as a *Jewish* mystic.

> Mystics are people who have vivid and typically frequent experiences of God, "the One," "the Sacred." Found in every culture known to us, they are also central to the Jewish tradition. In the broad sense of the word as I am using it here, the formative figures of the Hebrew Bible were mystics. Stories about Abraham, Jacob, Moses, Elijah, Elisha, and the classical prophets portray them as people for whom God was an experiential reality ... According to the gospels, he had visions, fasted, spent long hours in prayer, spoke of God in intimate terms, and taught the immediacy of access to God—something mystics know in their own experience. As a Jewish mystic, Jesus lived a life radically centered in God; that was its foundation.[8]

Borg points out that Jesus was also "a *healer*. Not all mystics become healers, but some do... More healing stories are told about

Jesus than about any other figure in Jewish tradition. He must have been a remarkable healer."[9]

Like mystics in other cultures, Jesus was known for his profound connection to the Holy in times of prayer, meditation, and solitude. That strong connection enabled Jesus to function as a link between two levels in our perception of reality; the transcendent healing power of God was made available to earthly, human brokenness. I am persuaded that heaven and earth are metaphors for two different dimensions or levels in our perception of a single reality. Jesus functioned like a shaman linking heaven and earth, one who brings divine healing and exorcism to those in need.

Mircea Eliade observes that shamanism is "pre-eminently a religious phenomenon," a form of mysticism found within a number of religions.[10] The shaman is, by definition, a medicine man who is "believed to cure, like all doctors, and perform miracles."[11]

Borg cites Luke: "But if it is by the finger [or Spirit] of God that I cast out demons, then the Kingdom of God has come to you" (Luke 11:20). Borg continues his explanation. "The passage joins Jesus's use of the Kingdom of God to the religious experience of a Spirit person [mystic]. Essential to a Spirit person's experience, as known through cross-cultural studies, are two tiers of consciousness, ordinary and extraordinary."[12]

Prayer, and especially prayer for healing, is a bridge between these two levels of perception. By God's grace, the healer is enabled to become an instrument of the transforming healing power of the Holy on behalf of a person who is ill.

THE KINGDOM OF GOD AS METAPHOR

From the time of Moses to Jesus's day, the term "Kingdom of God" was the language of metaphor, pointing to the realm of God's rule, power, and sovereignty, within humankind and the universe at large. This was always mediated through the spiritual experience of visionaries such as Moses, Elijah, Jeremiah, Isaiah, Jesus, and Paul. John Bright has observed that the human response called for over the centuries was always the same: the people of Israel are summoned to come into alignment with God's purpose in the world.[13]

The Kingdom, as Jesus explained it, is clearly a realm that is not separate from daily life. In the biblical worldview, heaven is a realm that informs every moment of our lives, but we may be unaware that this is the case. In Luke's Gospel, Jesus confers the Kingdom of God upon the apostles (literally, "the ones who had been sent out"). "You are those who have stood by me in my trials, and I confer on you, just as my Father has conferred on me, a Kingdom. (Luke 22:28–29).

The apostles were curious, wondering when the Kingdom would happen. We have an answer to their query in the Gospel of Thomas, discovered in 1945 in a field in Upper Egypt as part of the Nag Hammadi library.

> His disciples said to him, "When will the (Father's) imperial rule come?" "It will not come by watching for it. It will not be said, 'Look here!' or 'Look there!' Rather the Father's imperial rule is spread out upon the earth, and people don't see it." (Thomas 113)[14]

It seems to me that God intends to transform our awareness so that we can see the Kingdom "spread out upon the earth." God intends to transform our consciousness through the inpouring of holy love. God has lovingly made human beings to long for this transformation. And when human beings cooperate with God's intent, they enact the Kingdom of God.

New Testament scholar Elizabeth Schussler Fiorenza suggests that one way in which the Kingdom of God is enabled is through healing. "The earliest gospel strata assert again and again that Jesus claimed the *basileia* for three distinct groups of people: (1) the destitute poor; (2) the sick and crippled; and (3) tax collectors, sinners and prostitutes…The *basileia* of God is experientially available in the healing activities of Jesus."[15]

In our healing ministries, it is also available to us. How did Jesus heal as he and the disciples went about enacting the Kingdom of God? New Testament scholar John Dominic Crossan suggests that an altered state of consciousness is a crucial prerequisite for healing by a shaman, medicine man, priest, preacher, physician, or psychiatrist. He writes, "I emphasize as strongly as possible that Jesus was not just a teacher or preacher in purely intellectual terms, not just part of the history of ideas. He not only discussed the Kingdom of God; he enacted it and said that *others could do so as well*" (italics added).[16]

Crossan is persuaded that Jesus first healed the disciples, who then went on to heal others. Crossan bases his assumption on data from medical anthropologists who study the healing practices of indigenous peoples. It seems that Jesus expected his followers to offer healing to others as a crucial part of their mission of presenting the Good News of God to the countryside. Healing, then, is one important way that Jesus and his followers enacted the Kingdom of God.

"Jesus said to them again, 'Peace be with you. As the Father has sent me, so I send you.' When he had said this, he breathed on them and said to them, 'Receive the Holy Spirit'" (John 20:21–22).

In another context, Crossan asserts that those whom Jesus sent out were not a special group. "The missionaries were not some specific and closed group sent out on one particular mission at one particular time. They were predominantly *healed healers*, part of whose continuing healing was precisely their empowerment to heal others. I propose, in other words, a network of shared healing with Jesus."[17] Before and after his death, the healing ministry of his followers was, and still is today, a network of shared healing with Jesus.

The fact that Jesus commissioned his followers to carry forward his ministry and gave them authority to do so suggests that he taught them *how* to heal before he sent them out to enact the Kingdom of God. According to Matthew, Jesus gave the apostles his authority to heal and cure any disease. "Then Jesus summoned his twelve disciples and gave them authority over unclean spirits, to cast them out, and to cure every disease and every sickness" (Matthew 10:1).

In Jesus's day, healing included the casting out of unclean spirits who were thought to be the source of human illness. Consequently, exorcism was a method of treatment, a form of healing. As we look back two thousand years, the dividing line between exorcism and healing becomes very blurred. Both healing and casting out unclean spirits, though different in focus, restored wholeness and well-being to the one who suffered. Most healings were not related to a demon, but were a restoration to health. Both practices achieved the same goal.

EXORCISM AND HEALING

How is the Kingdom of God connected to exorcism and healing? John Wilkinson—physician, New Testament scholar, and senior fellow of the Royal College of Physicians in Edinburgh—suggests that exorcism is one of many methods of healing that Jesus used.[18] Other methods include healing by touch, speaking to one who was ill, applying saliva, and healing prayer at a distance. In healing by exorcism, Jesus addressed a word of command to the demons to leave:

1. The synagogue demoniac: *"Be silent and come out of him"* (Mark 1:25)

2. The Gerasene demoniac: *"Come out of the man, you unclean spirit"* (Mark 5:8, Luke 8:29)

3. The epileptic boy: *"Come out of him, and never enter him again"* (Mark 9:25, Matthew 17:18, Luke 9:42)

Borg suggests that a Spirit person not only works in two tiers of perceived reality but is also a "transmission line" of God's power between the two tiers. This two-tiered perception of reality comes directly out of religious experience. The phrase "on earth as it is in heaven," from Matthew's version of the Lord's Prayer, is a good example. As a devout Jew, Jesus understood his exorcisms as the active sovereignty of God, manifesting through him within the world of history. Borg observes, "His exorcisms were the 'power of the holy' entering the profane world."[19] The Kingdom of God refers to God's sovereign and enormously powerful rule of the universe. It is much more than a statement of belief, which is a common understanding of the term. To comprehend the Kingdom of God fully, one must *experience* this loving power that joins our perception of "heaven" and "earth."

Borg observes,

> In the exorcisms, that power "comes": "But if it is by the finger of God that I cast out demons, then the Kingdom of God has come upon you." The phrase "Kingdom of God" is thus a symbol for the presence and power of God as known in mystical experience. It is Jesus's name for what is experienced in the primordial religious experience and his name for the power from that realm which flowed through him as a Spirit person. Thus one may say that Jesus as a Spirit person experienced the Kingdom of God, a reality which, because it is ineffable, can be spoken of only in the language of symbols.[20]

Toward the end of the twentieth century, New Testament scholars such as Marcus Borg and Walter Wink broke new ground by insisting that it is not possible to understand the Kingdom of God unless the experiential presence of the Holy is acknowledged in the description, as it was with the visionaries in the Hebrew Bible. Wink describes heaven and earth as the inner and outer aspects or perception of a single reality.[21]

By its very nature, the "Kingdom" is ineffable and indescribable, so Jesus used a series of metaphors found in the parables to describe it. He saw healing as a manifestation of the Kingdom's presence. The healing practice that Jesus taught his disciples is set into the context of prayer, a loving experience of God's sovereignty expressed when another is in pain.

It has been my experience that preparing oneself to offer healing prayer to others is very effective when it is grounded in spiritual practices found in the contemplative tradition. Those practices enable us to be used as a conduit between "earth" and "heaven" for the operation of God's grace, allowing God's power to flow through us as it flowed through Jesus and through his disciples so many years ago. These spiritual exercises enable us to focus the mind and heart by paying pure attention to an icon, one's breath, a word or phrase, or a small object for ten minutes at a time. Such concentration is difficult because distractions flood into our awareness. But when we acknowledge the distraction and then bring the attention back again and again to an icon of Jesus, or the breath, our consciousness becomes more deeply centered and focused, so that God's power can better flow through when the healing prayer begins.

EXPECTATIONS OF HEALING: JESUS, PAUL, AND JAMES

Jesus's expectation about healing was similar and also somewhat different from those articulated by Paul and James. In his first letter to Corinth, Paul addresses the subject of healing in a different situation and context than Jesus and James were facing. Many of the Corinthian Christians were former Gentiles who had brought into that congregation's worship various ecstatic spiritual practices that sometimes caused members to disrupt worship. Writing to these Corinthians some twenty-five years after Jesus's death and resurrection, Paul described the gifts of the Spirit. "Now there are varieties of gifts, but the same Spirit…To one is given through the Spirit the utterance of wisdom, and to another the utterance of knowledge… to another faith by the same Spirit, to another gifts of healing by the one Spirit… All these are activated by one and the same Spirit, who allots to each one individually just as the Spirit chooses." (I Corinthians 12:4–11).

In chapter 13, Paul is concerned that some who claim to have the gifts of the Spirit have an inflated ego, a "noisy gong or a clanging cymbal." The authenticity of their gifts needed to be validated by the litmus test of love. The whole chapter, for Paul, focuses on testing the authenticity of spiritual gifts according to the presence of love. In contrast, although flawed motivation in the use of spiritual gifts was apparently a problem in the Corinthian congregation, neither Jesus nor James needed to test the validity of the people's motivation in employing the gifts.

Wilkinson suggests that the literal translation should be "'gifts of healings,' for both nouns are in the plural, although these gifts are given to one individual.[22] This is usually interpreted as meaning that there is specialisation amongst the gifts of healing with different gifts for different diseases, and that no one person could heal all diseases." The words *gifts of healings* are used by Paul only in the first letter to Corinth and in none of his other letters. The implication is that each individual who practiced healing in Corinth had a special gift to heal a particular disease. At the end of the chapter, Paul asks, "Do all possess gifts of healings? Do all speak in tongues?" (1 Corinthians 12:30). The implied answer is "No."

How were the gifts of healings used? Paul offers no advice, but if we are to judge from what we are told of his own healing practice in Acts 28:8, healing is offered in the context of prayer. "It so happened that the father of Publius lay sick in bed with fever and dysentery. Paul visited him and cured him by praying and putting his hands on him. After this happened, the rest of the people on the island who had diseases also came and were cured" (Acts 28:8–9).

According to Luke, the author of Acts, healing in the context of prayer was also practiced by Peter in curing Dorcas. "All the widows stood beside him, weeping and showing tunics and other clothing that Dorcas had made while she was with them. Peter put all of them outside, and then he knelt down and prayed. He turned to the body and said, 'Tabitha, get up.' Then she opened her eyes, and seeing Peter, she sat up" (Acts 9:40).

In contrast to Paul's delineation of various gifts in his letter to Corinth, Jesus believed that *all* of his disciples had the capacity to heal, and he expected all of them to offer it as needed. However, sometimes they were not able to heal and came to Jesus for instruction. (Mark 9:14–29). In later centuries, Paul's words about Corinthian gifts of healing turned into an unfortunate generalization: *only the specially gifted have the ability to heal.* That was not Paul's original intent. Unfortunately, that interpretation later became normative for much of the church. But it is quite different from Jesus's original instruction and expectation about healing.

Toward the end of the first century, the author of the book of James, who was a leader of the church in Jerusalem, addressed a letter to Jewish Christians living throughout the empire. In it he encouraged healing in the context of prayer. The letter reflects Jesus's original assumption that all of his followers are expected to offer healing.

> Are any among you sick? They should call for the elders of the church and have them pray over them, anointing them with oil in the name of the Lord. The prayer of faith will save the sick, and the Lord will raise them up... pray for one another that you may be healed. The prayer of the righteous is powerful and effective. Elijah was a human being like us, and he prayed fervently that it might not rain, and for three years and six months it did not rain on the earth. Then he prayed again, and the heaven gave rain and the earth yielded its harvest (James 5:14–18).

Dr. Wilkinson writes about this passage in *The Bible and Healing.*

> This paragraph provides one of the few glimpses into the healing practice of the apostolic Church that we have in the New Testament... We note first of all that its main subject is that of prayer. The key verse of the paragraph is found in verse sixteen in the words, "The prayer of the righteous is powerful and effective." The topic of healing is thus dealt with in the context of prayer. The intention of the author is to underline how prayer is the basis of all

the activities of the church, and its healing ministry is no exception to this.[23]

James teaches that the church is concerned about the sick. He takes it for granted that healing is part of the normal spiritual practice of a congregation rather than something unusual or extraordinary. Dr. Wilkinson continues,

> It was only with the rise and organization of the medical and nursing professions that the basis of healing moved out from the church to the community at large. It is this change that resulted in so much uncertainty in the church's attitude to healing and produced the tendency for the church to withdraw from its healing ministry or to identify it with the practice of certain procedures which are usually included in the category of "faith-healing."[24]

Dr. Wilkinson places strong emphasis on James's conviction. "Prayer is the basis of Christian healing when it is made in the name of Jesus Christ."[25] In the Jerusalem church of James, the elders had a role similar to that of leaders in a Jewish synagogue. However, all members of the congregation were urged to "pray for one another." According to Dr. Wilkinson, James does not mention the gift of healing.

> [James] appears to assume that all elders and even all members of the church can heal. His emphasis focuses on the place of prayer in healing, rather than on the special gifts of individuals. There need be no contradiction here. The presence of some with a special gift of healing does not mean that healing is necessarily confined to them, nor that all cannot share in healing.[26]

It can be inferred that James believes that each person has the capacity to pray with great effectiveness, for *"Elijah was a human being like us"* (italics added). The clear inference here is that our human prayers can be effective in the same way that Elijah's were. The author seems to be urging those in the church to offer healing even if they did not feel adequate. These verses point to the fact that healing in the Jerusalem church was available not just from a few specially gifted individuals but from the congregation as a healing community.

It seems evident that those who followed Jesus, and those whom he prepared to send out on mission, reflected his assumption that they all had the latent capacity to heal. It also seems apparent that he trained them to use various healing modalities grounded in prayer. After a period of time, they "got it," not because they understood the mechanisms of healing prayer but because they practiced it again and again. This observation is based on my experience in training more than nine hundred people to offer Christian healing. At Jesus's urging, healing began to happen in the apostles' mission. Jesus was a powerful role model and teacher of healing. He persuaded his followers that they actually had the ability to be conduits of God's healing grace, even though they may have not felt Jesus's charge.

WE ARE ALL HEALERS

In my experience as a teacher of healing, I have found that most of those who begin to practice healing prayer feel inadequate. My healing training is conducted in five-day retreats, each limited to a dozen participants. The most difficult thing for the students to accept is that each of them has an authentic capacity to be a surrendered instrument in God's hands for healing. Ultimately, these students did not learn to be effective instruments in God's hands because of the clarity of instruction, but because they practiced the prayer process again and again during the five days. The Spirit was present, and sometimes healing was observable. It seems to me that Jesus's followers probably learned to do healing in a similar way. In the retreats, the students are deeply touched by the experience and the power of the Spirit in both receiving healing for themselves and in offering healing to others again and again. During the five days of intense contemplative exercises and prayer, a spiritual force field seems to build in the group.

The most powerful healings that I have witnessed over the past thirty years have occurred in training retreats. Here is a letter from a participant early in 2002 (J. Koppel, personal communication).

> *You may recall at the workshop you held recently here in Portland that during the time of laying on of hands… you [and the group] prayed for my son David with me as a proxy for David. David had been diagnosed with multiple tumors (pancreas, spleen, small intestine, stomach lining, and right leg). Some were cancerous, some were benign. He has been undergoing weekly treatments for a couple of months… but many people have been praying for David as well. I have been very touched by the degree of compassion and caring that so many people have shown for David's situation. David had a monthly check up/status report with his oncologist this Wednesday. Guess what! All of the tumors are gone with the exception of three! Thanks be to God!! The three tumors that remain are on his spleen, however they have shrunk quite a bit and the doctor says there is no reason to believe, in the light of what has happened, that they won't go away too. I want to thank you for your prayers and the comfort they brought to me. While you and the others were laying hands on me on behalf of David, I could feel David's spirit, the warmth of his presence I give God the honor and glory and have an overflowing and thankful heart on the healing he has brought to David and that David realizes all the many prayers that have and are being said for him, and he knows it is God, working with the doctors too, that has brought to him body, mind, and spirit.*
> *God Bless… peace to you,…*

It is time to reexamine Jesus's original expectation that all of his followers could enable God's healing grace to unfold and see how Jesus's teaching applies to us. His followers were not aware that they had this latent healing ability. They simply lacked confidence in this undeveloped gift. They probably found it difficult to accept Jesus's way and model of healing and embrace the truth that each follower can be an instrument of God's spirit. Similarly, we may draw back, hesitate, assume that the gift resides in another and not in us. But the truth is that each person can invite this loving spirit into the heart through prayer and let it move out through the hands in healing. When people pray in Jesus's name, they invite his risen presence into the center of the healing.

Paul and James had very similar expectations about healing; the differences in their styles and emphases are minor. They both understood that God is the source and ground of sacred healing. They both urged others to offer healing. Each of them relied on prayer as the conduit for God's healing presence, and they invoked Jesus's presence.

THE HEALING STORIES

All the healing stories in the Gospels provide a fresh perspective on Jesus's interpretation and understanding of the various dynamics of healing. Mark recounts the following story, which illumines the importance of the ill person's attitude.

> Now there was a woman who had been suffering from hemorrhages for twelve years. She had endured much under many physicians and had spent all that she had; and she was no better, but grew worse. She had heard about Jesus, and came up behind him in the crowd and touched his cloak, for she said, "If I but touch his clothes, I will be made well." Immediately her hemorrhage stopped; and she felt in her body that she was healed of her disease.

Immediately aware that power had gone forth from him, Jesus turned about in the crowd and said, "Who touched me?" And his disciples said to him, "You see the crowd pressing in on you; how can you say, 'Who touched me?'" He looked all around to see who had done it. But the woman, knowing what had happened to her, came in fear and trembling, fell down before him, and told him the whole truth. He said to her, "Daughter, *your* faith has made you well; go in peace, and be healed of your disease." (Mark 5:25–34, italics added).

In this story, Jesus offers a radical new perception of faith as it applies to healing. The woman's faith was expressed by willingly accepting herself as a cooperating instrument of God's grace that can access healing. Jesus said, "Daughter, *your* faith has made you well." Jesus, by God's grace, not only cured the hemorrhage but also reintegrated her into the community that had rejected her because of her bleeding. She was no longer in violation of the law.

There is a spiritual hazard in this account because sometimes people turn the story in on themselves. If a person is ill and she prays, and others pray for her, but she is not healed, then a simplistic logic says, "My faith must be deficient because I'm not being healed." This pernicious, guilt-inducing form of logic assumes that every prayer is answered exactly in the way that it is asked. That simply is not the case, and we cannot know the reasons why some prayers are not answered in the way the person praying wants them to be answered. It is necessary to live faithfully in the mystery. We cannot know all of the variables that account for an illness, or for failure to recover from an illness.

Paul prayed that his "thorn in the flesh" might be removed, and three times the prayers were not answered. In response, Jesus said to him in a visionary experience, "My grace is sufficient for you, for power is made perfect in weakness" (2 Corinthians 12:7–10).

Paul had to learn to live with the mystery of why he was not healed. We need to understand that not every question has an answer.

We are called to live within the framework of God's mysterious creation. It can be gravely difficult to recognize that we may have no human control over outcomes. Prayer for healing is offered in cooperation with God's activity and grace; we make ourselves fully available to be an instrument of that grace, but we leave the results to God.

Paul's experience of not being rid of his thorn in the flesh is an example of the difference between *healing* and *curing.* The two terms are used interchangeably in the New Testament and generally mean the same thing. However, today, a helpful distinction is often made by some medical professionals. The root of the word *heal* goes back centuries to the concept of being whole. A person can be whole but not cured of an illness, as illustrated by Paul's thorn in the flesh. The distinction used today by many physicians would refer to Paul as "healed"—that is, his personhood was whole, but he was not "cured" the thorn was still there. (See further discussion of this distinction in chapter 8.

How should we view the healing stories in the New Testament? Are these accurate historical accounts of what actually happened, or do they sometimes reflect the theological agenda of the early church? Recent New Testament scholarship makes it clear that the various healing stories have different degrees of historicity. Addressing this issue, Marcus Borg observes that "The bible and the gospels (like the sacred scriptures of other religions) are human responses to the sacred. They tell us not what God says, but what our spiritual ancestors said."[27] He goes on to suggest that the Gospels "combine pre-Easter memory with post-Easter testimony… They combine memory and metaphor."[28]

Historical Jesus scholar William R. Herzog supports this point of view and cites John Meier's massive study of the historical Jesus[29] that contains a curious paradox.

> As an element in the Jesus tradition, exorcisms and healings are well attested. In fact, it is, historically speaking, a virtual certainty that Jesus performed mighty works that we call healings and exorcism…

The difficulty comes when interpreters move from their general conclusion about Jesus to the evaluation of specific incidents, the accounts of healings and exorcisms. None of these seem to pass the test of historical plausibility. So we find ourselves affirming, in general, that Jesus healed and exorcized but cannot credit any specific account of a healing or exorcism.[30]

Herzog suggests, like Albert Schweitzer before him, that the Gospels are collections of oral traditions put together by the Gospel writers. He says that every unit of oral tradition (called a pericope) doubtless had a history before it was used in the Gospels. Most likely, this history strongly influenced the text. [E]very text contained layers of tradition that had been laminated together to form the text as it appears in the Gospel narrative.… Let's look at the familiar story of Jesus healing the ten lepers (Luke 17:11–19). This story may have three layers of tradition folded into the text as we have it. At the core of the text is a healing story.

"core healing story   17:12–14   (the ten)"[31]

"As he entered a village, ten lepers approached him. Keeping their distance, they called out, saying, 'Jesus, Master, have mercy on us!' When he saw them, he said to them, 'Go and show yourselves to the priests.' And as they went they were made clean" (Luke 17:12–14).

Jesus tells the ten to go to the temple and show themselves to the priests to have their healing confirmed so that they would no longer be outcasts, excluded from the community.

"At the next stage of the tradition, one leper is singled out and distinguished from the rest. This is the first expansion of the story.

| "core healing story | 17:12–14 | (the ten) |
| "first expansion | 17:15, 16a, 17 | (the nine)"[32] |

> "Then one of them, when he saw that he was healed,
> turned back, praising God with a loud voice. He
> prostrated himself at Jesus's feet and thanked him.
> And he was a Samaritan. Then Jesus asked, 'Were
> not ten made clean? But the other nine, where are
> they?'" (Luke 17:15–17)

Jesus's questions

"change the status of the nine from faithful believers who trust
Jesus to heal them into ungrateful recipients of grace. Now the nine
are cast in a negative light. Why? What historical context or change
in the church's situation might account for the shift in emphasis?
One answer is that the church was struggling with the phenomenon
that many were being healed in their house church gatherings but
not many returned to become part of the community that healed
them. ...

"When Luke received these materials, he put them to yet another
purpose ...

"core healing story	17:12–14	(the ten)
"first expansion	17:15, 16a, 17	(the nine)
"Lukan expansion	17:11, 16b, 18, 19	(the one)"[33]

In this expansion of the story, Luke shifts the "previous emphasis
from the nine ungrateful lepers to the one grateful leper whom he
identified as a Samaritan."[34]

Herzog wonders why "Luke has transformed the grateful
Samaritan into a 'foreigner.' One possible answer is that Luke was
writing for a largely Gentile audience and may have used the healing
of the lepers as a paradigm for portraying the faith of outsiders
or Gentiles like those for whom he is writing. In this way, Luke

provides an opportunity for his audience to locate themselves in the stories of the Jesus tradition."[35]

Professor Herzog suggests that this text "may contain three distinct layers of tradition, each of which addresses a different issue."[36] He goes on to observe that the details of the healing stories "need to be analyzed circumspectly."[37] His observations support Borg's statement that "the Gospels are products of early Christian communities in the last third of the first century."[38]

Viewing the Gospels circumspectly does not invalidate the content of the stories, but only helps us to understand that all the healing stories must be viewed as a unit, in order to be seen as evidence that Jesus was a very powerful healer. The difficulty comes in analyzing individual stories that reflect changes and additions that come out of various early Christian communities in response to particular issues confronting them. Luke's three-layer story of Jesus healing the ten lepers is a good example of that process and addresses several issues but does not invalidate the extraordinary reality of Jesus's healing practice.

HEALING IN THE APOSTOLIC CHURCH

The disciples banded together after Jesus's death and his resurrection appearances to announce the Good News he proclaimed. They continued his ministry while they waited for the cataclysmic end of the world. Those in the next generation carried that ministry forward, but after twenty or thirty years, it became apparent that the world was not going to end in their time. In any case, the pattern of Jesus's ministry, which included healing, remained stable and was carried forward by the apostles. They continued doing exorcisms and healings because it met people's needs and came directly out of their experience with Jesus.

Jesus's risen presence was equated with the power of the Holy Spirit. Mighty acts were accomplished in his name. The term for these mighty acts, including healing, is sometimes translated in the Bible as *miracle.* The word *miracle* implies supernatural power as the source and points to the divine origin of the healer, the "miracle worker," and his/her God-given power.[39] In Matthew, Mark, and Luke, a miracle is viewed as a sign representing the activity of God in the world.

There is an account of a healing offered by Peter and John shortly after Pentecost. The author of Luke and Acts tells the story of a crippled man at the gate of the temple asking Peter and John for alms. The man looks expectantly toward them, and then the author records Peter's reply:

> "I have no silver or gold, but what I have I give you; in the name of Jesus Christ of Nazareth, stand up and walk." And he took him by the right hand and raised him up; and immediately his feet and ankles were made strong. Jumping up, he stood and began to walk, and he entered the temple with them, walking and leaping and praising God (Acts 3:6–8).

The use of Jesus's name invokes his presence and becomes the source of healing. This is illustrated as well by the account of a healing at Lydda. "Now as Peter went here and there among all the believers, he came down also to the saints living in Lydda. There he found a man named Aeneas, who had been bedridden for eight years, for he was paralyzed. Peter said to him, 'Aeneas, Jesus Christ heals you; get up and make your bed!' And immediately he got up" (Acts 9:32–34).

Today this traditional invocation is used in many denominations. An example is found in the order of "Ministration to the Sick" in the Episcopal *Book of Common Prayer*: "I lay my hands on you in the Name of our Lord and Savior Jesus Christ, beseeching him to uphold you and fill you with his grace, that you may know the healing power of his love."[40] I use a form of this prayer when anointing and laying on hands for healing. Sometimes when deep in prayer with eyes closed, it seems that others, invisible to the eye, are praying with me.

SUMMARY

In the biblical record, healing first emerges in the Mosaic covenant as God gives the assurance, "for I am the Lord who heals you" (Exodus 15:26). Apart from the Elijah/Elisha cycle of stories, individual healing of one person by another was seldom practiced in ancient Israel. However, God was perceived as the generalized source of healing. Jesus's unique embodiment of person-to-person healing was not a departure from, but a refinement of, the corporate faith of ancient Israel. Jesus's healing became a new way of expressing God's steadfast love for human beings who are not whole, who are often fragmented. Eugene O'Neill made this point very clear: "We are born broken. We live by mending. The grace of God is glue!"[41]

Jesus brought a new teaching and practice into the Judaism of his day. The new teaching was not only a set of ideas or concepts; it was also the *practice* of sacred healing that he must have taught his disciples. Jesus believed that healing was a sign of God's presence and that the Kingdom of God was at hand, manifesting at the very moment a person was healed.

CHAPTER 4

Integrating Healing into a Parish

I believe that grace's empowerment is present in all true healings, in deliverances of all kinds, and in any movement toward wholeness and love and freedom, however great or small. It is present in physical and psychological healing, in social and political reconciliation, in cultural and scientific breakthrough, in spiritual deliverance from evil, in religious repentance and conversion, and in the ongoing process of spiritual growth. It is present where love really grows. In every situation, grace enables us to make necessary initial changes and to continue, over time, to nurture those changes in creative, constructive ways.[42]

—GERALD G. MAY, MD

In each generation during the past two thousand years the church has sought to model its ministry, in one way or another, upon the practices of Jesus. Ultimately, the first-century Christians wanted to follow Jesus's own model of ministry, the one that he practiced and taught them during those precious few years he spent in their presence. This caring ministry is described in the Gospels, the book of Acts, Paul's letters, and particularly in the book of James.

Jesus proclaimed and explained the nature of God's compassionate sovereignty in what later generations have come to call the parables of the Kingdom of God. In the Judaism of his day, the practice of offering healing to others was not part of commonplace Jewish religious practice. Jesus made healing an original and significant part of the Good News of God that he proclaimed. Simon and his brother Andrew, James and his brother John, sons of Zebedee, could have had no knowledge of what the Kingdom of God was all about, or what to proclaim, or how to offer healing, unless Jesus had instructed them from the very beginning.

The disciples might well have been among the first people that Jesus healed, according to New Testament scholar John Dominic Crossan. He surmises that "the mission of those [disciples] healed by Jesus [was] to heal others. Jesus assumed no personal monopoly on exorcism or healing."[43]

In *Jesus: A Revolutionary Biography,* Crossan suggests, "They were predominantly *healed healers*, part of whose continuing healing was precisely their empowerment to heal others."[44]

JESUS CALLS TOGETHER A SPIRITUAL COMMUNITY

In contemporary language, Jesus called together a spiritual community, a band of "wounded healers." His mission and model of ministry was to send them out into the countryside in pairs with two major goals: first, to proclaim a new awareness of God's radical compassion that Jesus called the Kingdom of God, and second, to heal those in pain as an expression of that compassionate kingdom. In my view, the church at its best today is also a band of God's people who understand themselves to be a community of awkward helpers and wounded healers. Such an attitude helps prevent the church from becoming inflated by its own sense of importance as a carrier of Christ's presence and a conduit of God's healing.

The disciples who probably received healing from Jesus must have been enormously grateful to him for what had happened in their lives. Crossan reflects on this possibility:

To those first followers from the peasant villages of
Lower Galilee who asked how to repay his exorcisms
and cures, he gave a simple answer—simple, that is,
to understand, but hard as death to undertake. You
are healed healers, he said, so take the kingdom to
others, for I am not its patron and you are not its
brokers. It is, was, and always will be available to
any who want it. Dress as I do, like a beggar, but do
not beg. Bring a miracle and request a table. Those
you heal must accept you in their homes.[45]

Crossan suggests that the disciples were "healed healers" who
were to practice that skill and take the Kingdom to others. Is it
possible that Jesus's followers in the twenty-first century can become
"healed healers" and take the Kingdom to others? This book describes
one model of that possibility.

The original first-century model of healing in the Western
church's ministry began to recede in the fourth century, and the
practice of healing changed and was marginalized by the end of
the seventh century. For the past seventeen hundred years, Jesus's
healing ministries have been on the periphery in the life of the
Western church, not part of its core practice. The healing that Jesus
introduced to his followers could again become a vital ministry in
the mainline U.S. churches today. However, the subject of healing
is unusual and sometimes suspect by many people in mainline
denominations in the United States. One of the barriers is a common
stereotype created by some TV evangelists who present healing and
laying on of hands as a kind of religious show business, designed
to entertain the audience with immediate miracles. There is no
suggestion that healing can also be a process that may take days
or weeks, or even months. Everything about healing is explained,
and there is an answer for every question. The focus is often on the
personality of the healer, rather than the action of God. If that is the
only exposure to healing that a person has, then it becomes a barrier
and takes a good deal of effort to present a different model.

What holy work is the Spirit seeking to accomplish in the life of parishes in our time? I interviewed clergy and laypeople in five congregations where there are active ministries of healing. These interviews provide some examples that show how Jesus's healing ministry has continued into the twenty-first century.

How I view a parish has been influenced by my training as a spiritual director, with twenty years' experience walking beside individuals on their spiritual journey. In the sixteenth century, the Spanish mystic St. John of the Cross observed that the Holy Spirit was the real director in the relationship between an individual and a spiritual director. The director's task was then to discern and reflect to the directee his or her perception of what the Spirit was seeking to do in this person's life. It is necessary to bring that same question of discernment to the life of a parish: what work is the Spirit trying to accomplish in a particular community of Jesus's followers?

As one who seeks to carry forward Jesus's mission in the twenty-first century, I believe that the Spirit is seeking to do today what Jesus and his disciples did twenty centuries ago: to proclaim God's Good News and address the varieties of pain in people's lives. Jesus gave the disciples power and authority to cure diseases "and sent them out to proclaim the Kingdom of God and to heal" (Luke 9:1–2). Jesus's commission to his followers has not changed in two thousand years. In my view, and as Crossan suggests, the commission links together the proclamation of the Good News and healing as two primary elements of Christ's mission. The mainline Protestant church in the United States today certainly does proclaim the Good News in a wide variety of ways, but it has too often neglected the practice of healing as an integral element in that proclamation. One of my goals over the past thirty years has been to join others in the church who want to recover and expand Christ's healing ministry for our day. Healing is a skill that can be taught, learned, and practiced so that pain might be diminished and grace might abound. Over the past thirty years, it has been my privilege to offer healing training in numerous congregations on the West Coast to more than nine hundred people, a dozen people at a time.

Today, in the life of a dozen congregations on the West Coast that have received healing training, a variety of healing ministries have emerged. In these parishes, God's presence and the Spirit of Christ continue to address pain and stimulate wholeness through healing prayer and laying on of hands. I have interviewed individuals—clergy and lay—from six of these congregations. It becomes clear that they are beginning to experience instances of God's grace at work. Lives begin to change and transform. In some subtle ways, their prayer life in God is also beginning to change. God's grace touches those who receive healing, but it also touches those who offer healing prayer.

In another context, addressing the Global Council of the United Religious Initiative in Rio, William E. Swing, the Episcopal bishop of California, said, "No one can see spirit, but no one can disguise spirit. When the spirit is moving, the spirit has its way."[46] It seems clear that the work of spirit cannot be disguised.

The congregations that have received healing training vary in size from 2,000 members in a large urban cathedral to 140 members in a small-town church. Most of the people in the training have come from mainline denominations: Episcopal, Lutheran, United Church of Christ (UCC), Presbyterian, and so on. Training has also been offered in Unity churches.

Introducing a healing service into Unity congregations was no problem at all. Myrtle Fillmore, who co-founded Unity with her husband, Charles, in the late nineteenth century here in the United States, was a naturally gifted healer. She taught that healing was one of the foundation stones in the Unity School of Christianity. She realized that although we may not all be gifted in this area, nonetheless all of us are healers.

After the five-day training, many of the congregations have initiated a monthly healing prayer service or weekly or biweekly healing group. Some congregations offer healing stations with prayer and laying on of hands during or after communion in the sanctuary or a chapel, as part of the Sunday morning service. In all of these formats the individual who seeks healing comes to the healing station to receive prayer and laying on of hands.

WAYS TO INTEGRATE HEALING INTO A CONGREGATION

How does a pastor introduce and integrate healing into the life of a mainline parish? One barrier to accepting the validity of healing is that many people believe that spiritual healing is unscientific. A foundational assumption of our culture holds that science has an explanation for every phenomenon. If something like healing prayer cannot be explained scientifically, then it is unreal and has no validity.

If members of a congregation have never been exposed to a ministry of healing, introducing that subject can be a formidable challenge. In several mainline congregations, I asked the clergy how they introduced healing into the life of the parish.

WESTMINSTER PRESBYTERIAN CHURCH, PORTLAND, OREGON

Here are some excerpts from my interview on this subject with the Reverend Jim Moiso, then pastor of Westminster. The church has a membership of 750 people and had no previous experience of healing.

FG: Was there any resistance to introducing the healing ministry?

JM: I wrote a proposal for a monthly healing service and told the worship committee that I wanted to add an item to their monthly meeting agenda, but didn't tell them what it was. Because the idea of a healing service has such bad connotations in the minds of some people, I didn't want anyone to jump to conclusions. I had this written out, took it to their meeting and said, "Here is what I want." I asked them to think about it and pray about it. I said, "You don't need to decide anything for a month because it is too important to decide this in one meeting." We talked about it, how it might work, and what it might take to pull it off. I urged them to go down to Trinity Cathedral and attend their Taizé healing service on a Sunday evening to experience it. I told them, "I don't want you to vote yes because it's my idea. I don't want you to vote yes because Jim wants it. The only reason you can vote yes is because you believe this is where God is leading us."

So the next month we brought it back and talked about logistics and budget. There were no questions about doing it, particularly after a person who had been part of the church for seventy years said that he and his wife, who has Parkinson's and cancer, went down to Trinity. He said that he was so busy observing what was going on and taking notes that he almost missed it, but it was like a door had opened. I could have kissed him. For him to say that was very, very helpful. The committee said, "Sure, let's do it. This sounds like something we need to do."

We followed the same process with the Session. The committee took the recommendation to the Session, and again … "You don't get to vote on it this month. You only get to think and talk and pray about it. Here's how we think it can happen. Here's how we think it can be financed. Here is how the logistics will work, and we want you to go to Trinity Cathedral and try it." The next month the person who had been part of the church for seventy years came to the Session and told them that for him it was like "a door had opened." The Session unanimously said, "Sure we'll do it." They set aside ten thousand dollars as an endowment for two years.

FG: The process you followed was very wise, very open-ended, and full of freedom.

JM: I tend to be a process person, and I want to give people lots of space; otherwise, it's not worth doing.

FG: What you did is a marvelous model for introducing an unusual type of worship service that contains the difficult word *healing*. For so many mainline Protestants in the U.S., the word *healing* calls up images of the TV evangelist stereotype rather than a healing service set in the context of contemplative prayer, silence, readings, and Taizé chants. This is helpful for me and inspiring to see the Spirit at work so powerfully in your parish.

Westminster offers a healing service the third Saturday evening of the month modeled in part on a Taizé healing service held at Trinity Episcopal Cathedral across town. Jim Moiso introduced this healing service in 2001. Five years later, in April 2006, I received a letter from him that described the cure of a painful broken bone through prayer that lasted over a period of many weeks.

> *Our healing service continues. Not hordes of people, but each time, we know why we are there. God is indeed gracious. Our associate organist broke a bone in her foot last December. Twelve weeks later, still on crutches, not much had happened. Her doctor said he would do surgery—screws, etc. He had another doctor take a look at the X-rays. The other one detected what he thought might be a few new bone cells. His suggestion was to wait four weeks. Four weeks later, new X-rays: the bone was completely healed! She had been the object of pretty intense prayer. She was back at the piano playing for our healing service this month.*

ST. AIDAN'S EPISCOPAL CHURCH, SAN FRANCISCO

In 1988, the Reverend James Jelinek, rector of St. Aidan's Episcopal Church at the time, asked me to offer a healing training for members. (Jelinek went on to become the Episcopal bishop of Minnesota.) Since 1988, several trainings have been offered at St. Aidan's, and half a dozen individuals have taken the training in retreats at Wellspring Renewal Center in Mendocino County.

Healing ministry at St. Aidan's includes the following:

1. Prayer, anointing with oil, and laying on of hands during the main Sunday morning service.

2. During the 8:00 AM service, laying on of hands and prayers for healing are offered by members of the congregation.

3. A telephone/online healing prayer chain.

4. A healing prayer group that meets two Wednesdays a month in cooperation with St. Cyprian's Episcopal Church.

Intercessory prayer is, and has been, a significant part of the St. Aidan's culture over the years. My wife, Virginia, who is an Episcopalian, and I were active in the life of the parish from 1995 to 2004. The Right Reverend Bavi Rivera was rector from 1995 to 2004. In 2005, she became bishop suffragan of the Diocese of Olympia in the state of Washington. Here are some excerpts from my interview with her.

FG: How do you think a healing ministry influences the life of a congregation?

BR: I want to talk about St. George's in Salinas [California], where I served after my time at St. John's in Ross. At St. John's I participated in classes on healing that you taught in the late 1970s. We started a healing ministry at St. George's about four years after my arrival. One of the things that happened for me at St. John's was feeling a sense of powerlessness that changed into a sense of being able to harness or become an instrument of God's power. At St. George's the congregation moved to an identity of being a place of healing and intercessory prayer.

The other thing that I think in terms of the life of the congregation is that the healing ministry invites people into opportunities to gather in community for prayer. The prayer center isn't just in the liturgy or something you do by yourself.

FG: Do I hear you saying that the intercessory prayer and the prayer groups help to build spiritual community within the congregation?

BR: Absolutely.

FG: In other words, it somehow goes out by osmosis through the whole life of the congregation? It doesn't affect everybody, but it does affect a lot of people?

BR: Indeed. It also develops the pastoral care life of the congregation. An example at St. Aidan's was the folks who had AIDS. One young man was a friend of David Frangquist. He began to attend church, and we began praying for him. Some people in the congregation began to see that he had other needs, and they cared for him. It was primarily prayer, but he was very involved in the healing ministry. When his parents came to visit him, the healing ministry was very important to his mother. So this had a whole ripple effect in terms of pastoral care.

FG: Beautiful.

BR: The ultimate example of that was Oliver, who was part of the Wednesday night healing prayer group. When I challenged the congregation, telling them that he wanted to die at home, I said, "It is not going to be a really long time. We need to make this happen for him." The people who first picked up the ball were the people in his Wednesday night prayer group.

FG: So pastoral care by laity is influenced by the atmosphere and practice of healing prayer?

BR: Right, because like in the Epistle of James, you know all of a sudden you can't just offer prayer for someone and then walk away. You have to put your life where your words and your prayers are.

FG: Yes.

BR: It calls people into deeper relationships as well. When you have this healing prayer in the life of the congregation, it becomes a place where you can become more revealing about what is going on in your life.

FG: More transparency.

BR: Yes, because there is something that people can do about it.

FG: And they don't feel helpless.

BR: Right. The culture is such that one can say, "I'm hurting," or "I have cancer," or whatever. Healing prayer has provided the culture in which we can talk about these things. When I was called to St. Aidan's, I think it was David Frangquist in my interview who said, "Well, at St. Aidan's it's almost always true that someone is crying in the service, but it isn't always the same person." That whole ability to be able to cry, to be able to talk about what is going on in your life, that comes out of the fact that people have learned to do healing prayer. Healers say to someone at the healing station, "I pray for you, I lay hands on you." We have given them some ways to handle an inner burden, so the culture shifts.

FG: Yes, and people don't feel helpless, like they can't do anything. They also have the courage to ask God for what they need.

BR: Right, and that makes it more possible for people to be more open. I am reminded of a husband and wife in the parish who were going through some struggles with their marriage. They allowed their names to be placed on the prayer list, and both of them went to healing prayer on a fairly regular basis. I remember at their twenty-fifth wedding anniversary celebration the husband spoke about the tough times that they had had, and how the congregation had been there for them and allowed them to be who they were.

FG: This whole process gives the Holy Spirit an opportunity to work, not only in the personal lives of individuals, but also work in the larger life of the congregation.

BR: Exactly. I think that if the congregation believes in prayer, then the individuals learn how to believe in prayer. If the congregation believes in healing, then the individuals learn that they are in a culture that prays. It is an antidote to the fear that we have in our outside culture.

FG: This promotes and helps to deepen the congregation as a spiritual community. Because people are accessing the Spirit, they are praying. The Spirit is using them to promote wholeness and healing, and they are connected at a much deeper level to people who are hurting.

BR: Yes, it is also a place where someone can say, rejoice with me. A lot of congregations in the Diocese of Olympia have healing prayer ministries. And in the announcements, or at times in the service, people will stand up and say, "Rejoice with me. Give thanks with me because this wonderful thing has happened."

FG: Yes, so it becomes a spiritual family, a kind of extended family because of that openness, that transparency, that willingness to be vulnerable in community.

BR: Yes, indeed. The sense of the community is that it is a life of, in, and through prayer. That part which holds us together is prayer, part of what we do together is prayer, part of how we live is prayer. The healing ministry gives focus to that process that says, "This is part of what a Christian community does."

FG: It gives the Holy Spirit a scaffolding to work on.

BR: Right. And then it also gives people the freedom to be real because the healing prayer invites, almost demands, authenticity.

As clergy we sometimes struggle with the fact that two weeks after they have been home, we discover that people have been in the hospital.

FG: Yes, I've had that experience.

BR: We say, "Wait a minute, how come?" Well, that doesn't happen very often when the culture is committed; we pray for people before they go to the hospital. We lay hands on them before they have a certain procedure or surgery. The next piece that goes with that, it invites people into silence. One way that I helped to change the culture was that we waited until the healing was done before we went on to the closing prayer. That was the beginning of adding silence to the service.

FG: So the silence became a dimension of the larger practice of healing prayer?

BR: Yes. Because we had learned to experience silence after the healing in the service, we were able to introduce a time of silence after the lessons and after the sermon. It taught us how to be in communal silence, and it taught us to wait on God. One didn't have to say anything or do anything but just sit there and wait in the silence. I think there was an ability that came out of that to tolerate the silence and then later to invite the silence. At St. Aidan's that practice of silence came out of the healing prayer time.

FG: What sort of meaning does the practice of healing prayer have for you personally?

BR: I have to go back to St. John's in Ross in the early '80s. What it did for me was to give me a way of coping that I didn't have before. It was coping with the reality of this beautiful thirty-four-year-old woman being filled with cancer. Healing prayer was a way of saying, "Okay, there is a way to be in this world with something that awful." Without having to get stuck on the question "How does God allow something like that to happen?" I didn't get stuck there because God was saying, "Okay. Here is what we do." God became a partner in working through it, overcoming it, living with it.

FG: An ill person may not live, but they die well. They exhibit a kind of positive wholeness even though they are dying.

BR: I'll go back to the woman at St. John's. Three days before she died, we were sitting at her kitchen table. A bunch of us had gone up there to clean her house at her request. We had had communion together. Everybody else had left, and I was talking to her. She had stopped all the chemo at that point. She had been struggling with this for about three years, and I said, "I hate to see this happen to you." She said, "Oh Nedi, I could have been hit by a truck. In these years I learned to sail, I learned to fly, I did this, I did that. I've had this incredible life." She died with more than she had when she got sick. I think that part of her positive stance was our healing prayer and part was her own courageous attitude. She had a good death that I think was better than if she had died without her own prayers and ours. I was able to cope better as a pastor. It gave me a way to serve her again. It gave me something to do; it gave me a way to be there for her.

FG: And it gave you the strength of the Spirit to withstand the pain that surrounded you in the presence of a dying person that you cared about.

BR: Exactly. And it also gave me a community with whom to mourn when she died. I didn't have to do it alone. I was part of that healing community.

FG: That is the whole point of healing prayer, to invite and enable God—as best we can—to be present in that healing community. Our job as pastors and priests is to facilitate that.

BR: And we have companions on the journey. Part of the power for me and a lot of what I learned from you at St. John's and over the twenty years that I have been offering healing is teaching people that this process is not confined to clergy. This is a gift we all receive by virtue of our baptism.

FG: Right. That is a very important process. St. Aidan's is a fine example of lay people carrying out their baptismal vows and feeling that they are called to healing ministry. Healing ministry is not reserved to clergy alone.

From your experience at St. Aidan's, and as a bishop who shepherds congregations and clergy, how do you see the ministry of healing as a spiritual practice that can deepen and strengthen a congregation's relationship to God?

BR: One of the things we have been talking about is the whole sense of community, deepening prayer life. I think one thing about the practice of healing is that healing ministry is taking prayer seriously. It's living as though prayer makes a difference. And so what that means is living as though our relationship to God makes a difference, and cultivating that relationship makes a difference. It not only deepens the individual lives, it also deepens the congregational life. When we practice prayer together, the whole congregation's life is invested in sharing that process. When we do that together, we are living a life of trust. I think of trust as part of our whole relationship with the Creator. It is a sense of being part of Christ's ministry in the body of Christ and carrying on Christ's healing ministry. And then being the temple and the hands and the agent of the Holy Spirit. The real power of this is that it happens in community. There are special people who have gifts for healing, but even they call upon the community. One of the things any society needs desperately is to realize that we are not islands. We cannot do this healing process alone. The way we work with God is through each other. Part of what congregations have to give to the world and part of what they have to give to one another is the community of prayer, of healing, of relationship. Here is a place where people experience "I am my brother's keeper."

FG: In your pastoral role as a bishop, do you find congregations that could benefit from having healing ministries?

BR: Yes I do, but I rarely visit a congregation that does not have healing and laying on of hands as part of its ministry.

FG: Is that right? Is that just in the Northwest?

BR: I also think that healing has become part of the entire Episcopal Church.

FG: How did that happen?

BR: The old Prayer Book had prayers for healing and anointing done only by the priest. But then in the new Prayer Book of 1979, all those opportunities for ministries to the sick are right there. The theme of the new Prayer Book is "ministry belongs to the baptized."

FG: That comes through in the Prayer Book?

BR: We talk about how much more it still needs to come through, but it was so much a part of what the Prayer Book was trying to do and have happen. In the order of Ministration to the Sick it will say this or that part can be done by laity. That is the way it happened.

FG: Interesting history.

BR: So many of these healing liturgies and ministries we use today have their foundation in the 1979 Prayer Book.

FG: Is there anything that I haven't asked you that you would like to comment on?

BR: I talked about deeper trust. When we trust one another, we also trust God more, too, you know.

FG: What you have said here addresses the subtitle of this book, *The Congregation As Healing Community.* That is what you have been talking about.

BR: That is exactly it … and especially when you look at all the ways of talking about that. Not only is it the caring for, but it is also the walking with, and being with them in their pain.

FG: Thank you so much for sharing your penetrating insights and practical wisdom.

Bishop Rivera's observation about the side effect of healing prayer creating an atmosphere of openness is an important contribution to the life of a congregation that had never occurred to me before. The acclaimed heart researcher Dr. Dean Ornish has taught patients to reverse their disease. He observed that patients in his training program "need a sense of safety, a place where they can let down their walls and defenses and talk about what is really going on in their lives without fear that anyone is going to judge or reject them."[47]

Dr. Ornish found that this kind of openness accelerated the rate of disease reversal for his heart patients. A congregation that offers a place of safety becomes a healing community in more ways than one by its very quality of openness.

A MEMBER OF ST. AIDAN'S REMEMBERS

Patricia Brown was a member of St. Aidan's in 1988 when I offered healing training there at the request of the rector, James Jelinek. She leads the Wednesday evening healing group and has been part of the healing team from the beginning.

FG: You were a member of St. Aidan's when the first healing training was offered in 1988. How do you remember the introduction and integration of healing into the congregation following the training?

PB: There was serious interest in healing by some members of the congregation before the training was offered. The training became a focus for healing within the whole congregation. Not everyone followed through afterwards and continued to work on it, but healing became really valued within the congregation.

FG: So it strengthened and stimulated what had already begun?

PB: Yes. I think that Marilyn Jelinek's presence was an important part of that, too. [She was a nurse at the Student Health Service at the University of California at Berkeley.]

FG: It has been said that St. Aidan's is a congregation that takes prayer seriously. Assuming that to be the case, do you see any ways that this commitment to prayer has been influenced by the ministry of healing that has developed since 1988?

PB: Yes. One of the manifestations is the prayer chain. There has also been an increase in the number of trained healers who serve at healing stations offering prayer and laying on of hands at the 10:10 AM service on Sunday. Those healing team members are supportive of each other, and are supported by the congregation. Serving in the prayer chain helps to keep me in touch with the needs of the congregation during the week. I think this happens for other people, too. It is really wonderful to have healing be that important to the congregation.

FG: So it is in everybody's consciousness to know that healing prayer is available if they want it.

PB: Right.

FG: And they are willing to ask for it?

PB: Yes. It is always a wonderful surprise when someone who has shown no interest in healing comes back to a healing station.

FG: Yes. What meaning does the practice of healing prayer have for you personally?

PB: It is really important in my life, and it isn't just when I'm offering prayer at a healing station, but it has taught me to pray more and make a deeper connection with God and the community. This causes prayer to become more important in my life, and I feel like it has helped me heal enormously. It has been really important in my own healing to pray for other people.

FG: Did this realization develop over a period of time?

PB: It has emerged slowly over the years, particularly the last several years. The body work that I do feels like laying on of hands to me. One of the things that Peter Hayne used to talk about was when you put your hands on someone, imagine yourself against the wall behind you and that God is right there working right through you. I always remember that. I'm not doing the work. I'm just a channel for God. What a gift for me to be able to do that. To be willing to stand back is important.

FG: On Sunday mornings as a healer you have listened to many prayer requests from people before you pray with them and lay on hands. How do you think the Spirit is at work in those requests and in your prayers and in the prayers of the support people who pray silently and lay on hands from behind?

PB: One of the things in my belief around healing is that we need to ask for it. We need to be open to be healed. And I think that anyone who stands up and chooses to come back to a healing station has made that choice. For me I don't think it matters to know what we need healing for. We don't always know what we need. What the person asks for I always address in my prayer, but that may not be the healing that is going to happen right then. I feel that the support people who are standing behind the one receiving prayer… their silent prayer and laying on of hands are as important as my verbal prayer and laying on of hands. It is a group process, a group healing.

FG: Sometimes when offering healing, I can almost feel the spiritual energy of the support people as well as the spiritual energy of the two assigned healers who anoint, pray, and lay on hands.

PB: Yes, and it used to be that we always didn't have a big support group. Now there is a group of five or six people who come back to the chapel regularly to give prayer support.

FG: The main parts of the healing ministry at St. Aidan's are people coming back to the kneelers at the Icon Chapel during the 10:10 AM service on Sunday, the prayer and laying on of hands by the congregation at the 8:00 AM service, the prayer chain, and the Wednesday evening healing group. In addition to that, prayer is asked for individuals whose names are read aloud in the two morning services. How do you think that kind of multifaceted healing ministry influences the larger life of the congregation?

PB: I think that new people coming into the life of the church become aware that healing is valued by the congregation, that this is a community that believes in healing, and that it is valued by people who don't participate in healing.

FG: What would you like to say about the ministry of healing at St. Aidan's that I haven't asked you?

PB: I think that having a healing ministry makes prayer more important in the life of the congregation. It isn't just coming to church on Sunday. For St. Aidan's people, prayer becomes an integral part of their lives.

FG: When you share with friends outside of the church that you are part of the healing ministry here, what kind of reaction do you get?

PB: I have a friend in her eighties who is a professed atheist. Twice when someone in her life that she cares about was sick, she showed up in our Wednesday healing prayer service.

FG: Oh, is that right?

PB: Yes, it was so incredible to me that when she was worried, she was willing to pray and have other people pray.

FG: And she was caring about a friend?

PB: Yes, and that prayer might help. She is such an old curmudgeon that when she called and asked me about coming to the service, I held the phone out and looked at it and said to myself, "Is this possible?" Because she is not a person who believes in prayer at all.

FG: When you look out across the other Episcopal churches that you know—some have a healing ministry and others don't pay much attention to it—what would you like to see happen in the Episcopal Church to deepen a ministry of healing?

PB: I think the new bishop might make a real difference. If this bishop valued healing and put it out there, if he thought the priests ought to encourage it, it would definitely change things for a bishop to be supportive of lay healing.

FG: Right. Where would you like to see the Spirit at work in the future of St. Aidan's ministry of healing?

PB: Lay Eucharistic Ministers take communion to everyone who is sick. I think everyone on the healing team should be doing that. I feel that when I take Eucharist to a shut-in, that I'm bringing the community and God, that I'm giving them what I've received. That is an important part of healing.

FG: Is there anything you would like to say about healing before we close?

PB: Yes. Healing has changed my life. I think I felt very isolated until I got into healing, that I didn't feel part of the universe, that I was an individual person only. I found it in my painting before I found it in healing. All of my paintings are healing for me because I'm being connected to the universe, being connected to God, that I'm opening up and up to be part of the whole. My faith in God used to be that God was somebody up there and not here, present, and active in our lives. God is in me and the people around me.

FG: And that the Spirit was doing the healing that was happening?

PB: Healing happens when you think that.

FG: So you lost a sense of isolation and being distant from the universe and other people?

PB: I was a member of the church, but I was an *individual* member. Do you know what I mean?

FG: Yes, you felt that you were not an integral part of the community. Thank you so very much, Patricia, for this interview and for your contribution to the book. Our readers will be helped by your experiences, observations, and insights.

Though one out of five verses in Matthew, Mark, and Luke deals with healing, introducing and integrating the practice of healing into a mainline congregation today is often a challenge. Clergy and laity in the two congregations described above have responded creatively to that challenge, using a variety of healing models. In each congregation the ministry of healing influences and permeates the spiritual life of the parish. It is clear to me that the Spirit is doing its work in both congregations.

CHAPTER 5

Healing Transforms Clergy

The individual sees God and embraces Him. And yet the individual is not a whole, but a part. "Every man has a light over him, and when the souls of two men meet, the two lights join each other and from there goes forth one light. And this is called generation." To feel the universal generation as a sea and oneself as a wave, that is the mystery of humility.[48]

—MARTIN BUBER

Over many centuries and in many parts of the world, pastors, priests, shamans, religious, and rabbis have prayed with their people when they were ill, burdened, or in pain. Clergy who have participated in the healing training and who follow a regular practice of healing prayer for others often discover that this practice is transforming in their own lives. It often changes them and sometimes those with whom they pray. Much of the time when praying for a person's healing, one has no way of knowing if the prayers make any difference. It is necessary for healers to believe that they make a difference, to take it on faith that God uses the people who pray, and to not be overly concerned about any measurable results.

As I observed earlier, I learned a deeper way of praying for healing from a research psychologist, Dr. Lawrence LeShan. LeShan was not a pastor, priest, or rabbi, but a man of profound spiritual depth who developed a healing method after studying healers in the United States, England, and India.

LeShan also studied spiritual practices from several of the world's religions that he made part of his healing method. They are described in his book *How to Meditate*.[49] He sifted out the common factors in the healing methods that he had learned from the healers that he interviewed. Some of the healers did not use the word *prayer* to describe the spiritual bonding that occurred when healing happened. LeShan did not often use the word *prayer* but was supportive of my use of the word when advising me in the writing of my 1981 doctoral dissertation, "Healing Training in the Church."

LeShan taught his students not to be preoccupied with the ultimate outcome of healing because the little ego would become attached to the results. This would block the healing process of spiritual bonding. As a pastor praying with someone in pain I find it difficult not to become preoccupied with results because so much is at stake. LeShan insisted that in the process of bonding or merging with the subject, the healer needs to become preoccupied with just one thing—love for the person in pain—and let the results happen as they may. The healer cannot control the result because there is a larger process at work that is beyond understanding. He was fond of quoting Agnes Sanford, who said, "Only love can generate the healing fire … when we pray in accordance with the will of God."[50]

Some years ago I served as an interim pastor for a United Church of Christ congregation in the Central Valley of California. A boy in one of the church families was riding his bicycle to school one morning when he was struck by a car and suffered a severe head injury. He was in a coma for nearly a week. I visited him each day in the hospital, spoke to him as if he could hear me, and prayed with him from a very deep level of my being. In a one-sided conversation with him, I knew that at a conscious level he could not hear me. A physician friend had told me some years earlier that, at some level below ordinary consciousness, a patient in a coma could absorb every word that was said. Members of his family and friends visited him and prayed with him daily while he was in the coma. He made a complete recovery.

About six weeks later, he asked me if he could say a few words to the congregation in the Sunday service. He told us that he could remember some things while he was in the coma, some words in the prayers that had comforted him. He thanked those who had prayed with him during those hospital visits.

At the time we were praying, we, of course, did not know whether he could hear us. We had to take it on faith that God was acting in his injured body through our prayers and the prayers of many others. His words of appreciation to the congregation made a deep impression on me and validated my leap of faith that God could use our prayers to comfort and to accelerate healing. His words of thanks were a great gift to me because after that I was more certain than ever that God could and did use my prayers and the prayers of everyone who loved him. His words of thanks changed me, increased my confidence, and deepened my faith.

WESTMINSTER PRESBYTERIAN CHURCH, PORTLAND, OREGON

It has been my experience that the prayers for healing that are offered for others as a regular practice often change the one praying. The following excerpts from interviews with clergy bear this out. Jim Moiso was the pastor of Westminster Presbyterian Church in Portland, Oregon. I have quoted from my interview with him in chapter 4. Here is an excerpt from a different part of that interview.

FG: What meaning does this healing practice have for you personally?

JM: It's really changed my ministry. I have an awareness of a part of myself spiritually that was there but I was not nearly so in tune with. This is not wholly new, but rather a kind of blowing open something that may have been latent for a long time. This started prior to the healing training. It began with my wife's encounter with cancer and my praying around that illness. This has added a powerful dimension to my ministry. I see what I do now, through brokenness and healing, more clearly than I ever have. It is a lens that is here all of the time. It may have existed before, but I wasn't so aware of it. Also, that lens is present when I think about who God is and what God intends. I'm much more conscious of that than I have been. In some sense I am more deliberate about it. These monthly healing services we do, in terms of worship, are the most powerful worship I experience.

We have been at this for about two years. It is not as scary as it was at first, but it is at least as awesome. I shake my head and ask myself, "How come I get to do this?" It feels like an immense privilege to me, and that has not diminished over time. I'm just sort of boggled by the fact that we get to do this. We get to, somehow in our halting way, be these vehicles for God. And it does make a difference to other people.

FG: Has it influenced your preaching in any way?

JM: Oh yes, I think there is more authenticity. It comes through from underneath, and there is more encouragement for me to trust in God. What people have told me over the past few years is that my preaching is getting better and better. What that means to me is that I am connecting more. It doesn't mean that I'm getting better, but there is more meaning for them. They are getting into it better.

FG: They are getting nourished at a deeper level?

JM: I think that is what is happening. Obviously it is all tied up in Linda's illness [his wife] and death because that has broken me open in some ways that never would have happened otherwise. It has all happened at the same time. With all that life experience, with all that living on all those levels, I'm different. The best compliment a parishioner can give me is "That sermon was helpful."

Last year somebody from one of the hospitals wanted to start a healing ministry and wanted to talk to me about how to do it. We discussed it, and essentially what I said was

"We didn't go looking for this. It wasn't as if we looked at everything we were doing and said, 'What's missing in our programming for people?'" It found us essentially through Linda. It really came to us. I suspect that we resisted it for a while because it was so unusual and scary. I don't know if that is true for other groups; I just know it's true for us. This was not something we sought. It found us, and we had to do something with it.

FG: It sounds like the work of the Spirit again.

JM: It is for me, and that is what I tried to say to that hospital person. For me it was something we could take the risk of doing and that we needed to respond to. Somehow I think that God really came to us and said, "This is a gift for you."

In the healing practice, Jim Moiso discovered a deeper part of himself that brought some changes to his ministry. It was a part that was not wholly new, but deeper. He sums it up in two words: "I'm different." The clarity of his insight and self-awareness that came out of his deep prayer and painful life experience was transforming and quite moving.

UNITY IN ASHLAND, OREGON

The Reverend Sherry Lady was the minister of Unity in Ashland, Oregon. Before that, she was on the staff of Unity in the Valley in Eugene, Oregon. She has been practicing this form of healing for about four years and has taken the advanced healing training. She is now teaching contemplative healing with her friend and colleague, the Reverend Inge Tarantola, minister of Unity in Roseburg, Oregon. They teach healing to Unity congregations in various parts of the country. Here is an excerpt from my interview with Sherry Lady.

FG: As a person who has been part of this ministry and has been through several trainings, what kind of value and meaning does it have for you personally?

SL: It is of great value to me. When I'm visiting people in the hospital, I have learned to listen to people and to be centered with them, present with them. I feel I have more confidence. If I am personally in the right space, then I can be more effective. I think it has helped me become more aware when Spirit is moving.

FG: Yes, you are more aware of when it is and when it isn't.

SL: Right, my ego wants to be Agnes Sanford! I want to have a high level of spiritual experience, and there are times when I do. I would not have known about that if it had not been for this training.

FG: Since your training began four years ago, do you feel that your ability to be a conduit of God's spirit and healing has deepened?

SL: Yes, though in previous years I also thought that healing was possible, but I never paid attention to it.

FG: Does it influence your counseling or preaching?

SL: I think that it influences my counseling. It has an inner effect on me when I am delivering a sermon. I think there is increased authenticity. I don't know how to explain that. When you're in the space and in your most authentic connection to God, you can get yourself out of the way. Then the work is done in me as well as the people I'm working with. That has been the benefit for me.

FG: Wonderful. You've mentioned earlier that team members often feel more centered and more present when doing a hospital call. I'm assuming that would be the same in counseling. You can be an instrument of healing even though you are not setting out to do a healing. But there is a level of focus and centeredness where Spirit can assist.

SL: Yes, and confidence that my faith is really working. It is confidence that when you get into that space, and when you are open, confidence comes from an inner knowing. Rather than, well, somebody else knows, but not me. So I'll be quiet over here in the corner.

FG: It is sort of losing that reluctance to speak up.

SL: Yes, that is a good way to put it.

FG: Thank you so much for your insightful answers to my questions and for the healing ministry that you have helped to fashion in two congregations.

PEACE LUTHERAN CHURCH, DANVILLE, CALIFORNIA

The healing ministry has been part of the spiritual formation of the pastor and laity in the Peace Lutheran Church parish over a period of fifteen years. Peace Lutheran Church is a congregation of about five hundred members in Danville, a suburb in San Francisco's East Bay. Pastor Steve Harms is encouraged by the healing ministry because he can better see his work as part of the larger work of the Spirit. He senses that the healing ministry influences the whole church.

FG: What value and meaning does this ministry have for you personally?

SH: It both allows and encourages me to see my work as participating in the greater work of the Spirit and not feeling I have to carry the responsibility all of the time, which is a dangerous trap. Clarifying that is very significant for me. It is a sharpened awareness of what is my work in the situation and what is the work of the Spirit. It is the most profound gift unfolding in me. First, I'm so busy, and second, I'm such a pragmatic "problem fixer" that I want to jump in there and get at it. The grace of healing prayer is allowing me some breathing room and encouraging me to be aware of the presence of the Spirit in events happening to me on a regular basis.

FG: Do you see anything happening in the life of your congregation that can be attributed to the healing ministry over the years?

SH: The healing prayer ministry is the bedrock foundation of congregational life. It is very subtle. In some ways it is forming the spirit of the congregation. The healing prayer team is a very substantial influence in our life together. Two or three individuals on the team have deepened their spiritual journey and life of prayer as recipients of healing. There have been dramatic shifts in their self-understanding, and, through the struggles in their lives, they are growing. Participation in the healing ministry impacts their sense of self.

In early December of 2002, with war clouds on the horizon, we held interfaith services for peace. The healing prayer team participated in that. Last Sunday we observed the birthday of Martin Luther King Jr., and my sermon addressed healing of the social dimension. Three times a year we have healing prayer as the theme of the Sunday service. There are four kneelers around the chancel and one in the gathering hall. Last Sunday the associate minister took children to a separate place for healing prayer both in receiving healing prayer and offering it. The children have participated in the healing stations before.

FG: It sounds like the children really get it. Do they respond more openly?

SH: The children are fully engaged. Sometimes six or eight kids are praying with the healing team at the kneelers.

FG: So the healing ministry has been pretty well accepted?

SH: There is great receptivity, but also a lingering doubt for some because of TV faith-healing programs people have seen.

FG: Are some people shy about coming forward for healing in the service?

SH: Later in the week after a healing service, a person might say to the pastor, "I didn't come up for healing because I'm in a tender place, and if I did, I might fall apart."

Several months later, Pastor Steve Harms called to tell me about a new development in the work of the healing team. He had asked members of the team to pray for the well-being and highest good of the congregation throughout an entire Sunday service.

FG: When did this new prayer process start?

SH: We began this in Lent and asked the healing prayer team to become the core for this experiment. It has been an incredibly powerful experience for each of those participating. There has been a shifting, altering in worship as well.

FG: How did that manifest?

SH: The atmosphere in worship is… the best word I can come up with is… *thicker.* I sense an enriching and deepening happening. The team members who are offering prayer throughout the service are really charged.

FG: Do they pray through the whole service?

SH: Yes, with the exception of the Eucharist. They sit in the back section of the sanctuary. We put a notice in the bulletin when this began, saying that you may notice that some people seem not to be participating in the service, but they are praying for the well-being and highest good of the congregation during the course of the service. They simply remain in prayer and are not completely invisible.

FG: So they do not become the focus of attention.

SH: Exactly. Then they do participate and receive the Eucharist.

FG: How many team members per Sunday usually?

SH: We have been experimenting. There are some who do it singly and others, two people. I can't say a preference has arisen yet, but both are valued. A decision has now been made to spread that out to other folks in the congregation who are also people of prayer. So a few more are being asked beyond the prayer team.

FG: So you are continuing it past Lent?

SH: I always bring these experiments up for evaluation and review. It has been a screaming success. Oh yes, oh my. It has deeply moved members of the team who are praying, and they report going into a very deep state of prayer. Connections are being made from the heart to the community as a whole. I am aware of, and have an intense regard for, the brokenness and the beauty in people's lives that I sense in the service.

FG: This is an exciting development.

SH: It is, and when the idea came to me, it was the healing prayer team that I was able to turn to. That is the other pivotal thing. It made the possibility real. There is already context and understanding among them, and finally, even the immediate conviction about it.

FG: Do the members of the team report a very positive experience in addition to what you and others sense in the congregation?

SH: Absolutely. We met late in the Lenten season to evaluate and discuss this process. It is very moving for prayer team members. Though it was scheduled to end at the close of Lent, they don't want to stop. This was not even up for debate. So we are continuing this prayer process of having one or two people pray for the well-being and highest good of the congregation during the course of the service.

FG: Your experiment with this prayer process during the Sunday service seems to provide the Spirit with an opportunity to do its work in the life of your parish. Thank you for sharing this process with me.

UNITY IN THE VALLEY, EUGENE, OREGON

Baine Palmer introduced himself to me after a Taizé healing service at Trinity Episcopal Cathedral in Portland, Oregon, in the fall of 1999. He asked me to offer a healing training for a group from his congregation, Unity in the Valley in Eugene, Oregon. Because he is a Unity minister, healing is part of his tradition. He had a few experiences as a gifted healer before we met. Here is an excerpt from my interview with Baine Palmer.

FG: What value and meaning does this healing ministry have for you personally?

BP: I believe in the power of prayer, so I move forward myself as people pray with me. Receiving prayer for myself and offering prayer with others assists me in my own spiritual development. It also assists me in leading this church. On occasion I have come to the Monday night group and asked to be a proxy for the church. I pray for my own healing spiritually, and I pray for wisdom in knowing how to lead.

FG: Right, right.

BP: I've had experiences of praying in which three people have come out of comas. Nobody really knows about this. I just pay attention to where I should be. When I think that I'm supposed to be present somewhere, I'll be there.

FG: Tell me about people coming out of comas.

BP: There was a boy about nine years old in Memphis who went into a coma for three days. They could not find out why. I was in Memphis seeing the family. I just got this intuitive hit that I was supposed to pray with him. I asked the family if I could be alone with him. I just laid my hands on him and allowed the healing activity of God to move through me into this child. Then I left. He came out of the coma about an hour later.

FG: Beautiful.

BP: Another experience, my nephew was in a head-on car crash with head injuries in a Birmingham hospital. I went down there. Intuitively I was guided again because though he had head injuries, he was not brain damaged. Again I just laid my hands on him and told him that the healing activity of God was moving in him and through him. He awakened later that day.

FG: Remarkable.

BP: We had a man here in Eugene who went into a coma. A woman from the church and I happened to be present in the hospital room at the same time. The woman stood at his feet. I put one hand on his head and one hand on his heart and prayed. He woke up that night.

FG: Yes, awesome.

BP: That is so sacred. If it is a gift and I'm supposed to use it, then I believe that I will be shown how to use it. It's almost like I know when and when not to offer healing. I just pay attention to that intuition. I've never told anybody what I just told you. There is just a handful of people who know that.

FG: Yes, this is a gift that you share with others under certain circumstances.

BP: So I did exactly what we do in laying on of hands in the healing service.… I didn't do the exercises beforehand, like focusing. But I was focused.

FG: Yes of course, you were.

BP: I just laid my hands on him and had faith that God could heal him.

FG: Thank you so much, Baine. This is very, very helpful.

Baine Palmer is aware that being healed himself is an important influence in his leadership of the congregation. His gift of healing with people in comas was present before he took the healing training.

CLERGY EXPERIENCE PERSONAL TRANSFORMATION

It has been said that we live in a world of specialization and that the pastor is one of the few remaining generalists among the professions. Being a generalist in an age of specialists is a challenge. Like a general practitioner in medicine, the pastor needs to know a little bit about all the specialties. Within Christianity, prayer might be called a specialty.

Whether clergy or lay, any person who follows a regular spiritual practice will change and grow toward what God intends him or her to be. Contemplative healing is a powerful spiritual discipline that is particularly effective for clergy who want to cooperate more effectively with the movement of the Spirit and be more open to God's presence in the congregation and in their own lives. All four of the pastors interviewed here agree that the practice of healing has changed their ministry. Using different metaphors, each describes a deepening of their relationship to God, and each has become more aware of how the Holy Spirit works in their lives. They sense that not only have they changed because of their healing practice but their preaching has also changed. For Jim Moiso it was "more authenticity." Sherry Lady describes "an inner effect on me when I'm delivering a sermon… increased authenticity."

These interviews reveal that all the pastors have experienced spiritual growth as a by-product of their practice of healing prayer. Jim Moiso describes the practice as "blowing open something that may have been latent for a long time." Sherry Lady has "become more aware when spirit is moving… I think that it influences my counseling." Baine Palmer senses that "receiving prayer for myself and offering prayer with others assists me in my own spiritual development… and in leading this church." Steve Harms is clear that the ministry of healing "has sharpened my awareness of what my work is in the situation and what is the work of the Spirit."

Many of the pastors express gratitude for being able to participate in the ministry of healing. Jim Moiso said that the practice of healing prayer "feels like an immense privilege to me… it's really changed my ministry." Sherry Lady experiences it as "confidence that my faith is really working." Steve Harms senses that the practice of healing prayer has not only changed him personally, but "in some ways it is forming the spirit of the congregation" and is "a very substantial influence in our life together."

All the pastors interviewed describe how they were personally moved and transformed by God's grace in their practice of healing.

CHAPTER 6

Laity Experience Transformation in Healing

The approach to the numinous is the real therapy and inasmuch as you can attain to the numinous experiences you are released from the curse of pathology. Even the very disease takes on a numinous character.[51]

—CARL JUNG

Lay people as well as clergy who participate in the healing ministry often become aware that they are transformed and changed by the experience. Healing prayer becomes a spiritual discipline for them. Any spiritual discipline followed on a regular basis brings change, but the healing discipline influences one's spiritual formation in particular ways. As Jesus was the man for others, so, too, are those who practice healing prayer. Following this discipline of prayer puts one's own life in better balance and brings greater inner harmony. Those who serve others are not so preoccupied with their own agendas. When you offer healing prayer on a regular basis, you can see God's grace at work in the loss of pain and sense of support experienced by those for whom you pray. Many laity report that following such a discipline is enormously rewarding.

Chris Huntze is a member of Peace Lutheran Church, mentioned in chapter 4, and has been part of the healing team for a number of years. He was particularly moved when he observed children coming forward to ask for prayer. Here is an excerpt from my interview with him.

FG: What was it that caught your attention about the children asking for prayer?

CH: It brought tears to my eyes to see an eight-year-old child kneel and have the opportunity and sense of being safe, to be able to pray openly in the community with fifteen or twenty people around.

FG: Yes, indeed.

CH: I think that is such a beautiful way for a child to grow up in his or her faith community. That is what has influenced me the most. Just to see an eight-year-old kneeling, with a group around laying on hands, saying, "Please pray for Grandma or my friend who has cancer." What that did for me was to remember that I didn't have that kind of experience as a child—which I would have liked to have had. What I think has been the most beautiful experience for the congregation is to see the openness of these children who are able to pray.

FG: That gives you hope for the future, I suppose?

CH: Twelve or fourteen people have taken the training and become part of the healing team. Two people who came back from the training last summer were glowing for two weeks. They were amazed, grateful, just on fire. These two have moved to a new level of gratitude. They just appreciate the relationships they have with the people in the congregation. They feel it is an honor to pray with them, and they see it as a privilege. They enjoy doing it. Steve [the pastor] asked members of the healing prayer team to do what he calls "Prayer at the Pew." He asks one person to pray during the entire worship service, invoking and inviting the Spirit to be present for the highest good of the people who are worshipping. We did that during all the services in Lent this year. I was able to do it twice, and it was powerful. It was a trip! I chose to sit on the perimeter of the congregation praying through the entire service. I did not sing the hymns or stand up, except I did take the Eucharist. Other than that, I was in a state of contemplative prayer during the entire service.

It was quite an experience. You are conscious of everything going on around you. You are listening, but you are praying and inviting the Spirit. You are on this journey with the others. It was just really cool. I was so enriched by that hour and a half of meditation and prayer, calling the Spirit to hold everyone in the congregation during that time.

FG: My, that must have been wonderful.

CH: So, in a sense, it was compatible with the practice of healing prayer. Other people on the healing team reported a similar experience when they did it. We were just asking for the Spirit to come to everyone and infuse every atom in the room. I felt like we became an extended family in that experience. The word that comes to mind to describe the experience is *reverence.* I think that offering prayer throughout the worship service has really enriched the folks on the healing team. It is wonderful to see people come back from the training retreats with that renewed vigor.

FG: Do you feel that God's presence is more available to you as a result of your participation in the healing ministry?

CH: Definitely. I think that is because of the regular practicing. It seems that the prayers come more quickly when I'm in church than in other places. I think that is a positive benefit of the practice. The more you do it, the better it becomes.

FG: Is there anything that I haven't asked you that you would like to add?

CH: When I participate in assisting someone with their prayer, do I feel like there is anything that rubs off or stays with me? Yes. Every time I have been at a kneeler and someone comes and I've helped them send their prayer, I feel nourished and enriched. It's almost as if we're acting as a conduit; the prayer comes through and leaves part of it in us.

FG: Yes, I've had that experience also.

CH: I'm just energized for hours after doing it. Just being around that other person and sharing in their prayer and sending it off is personally so enriching. That is almost a selfish thing.

FG: You don't do it for your own pleasure, but you do receive a by-product that is very, very rewarding.

CH: Yes, a by-product that keeps drawing me to the practice because it feels so good.

Greg and Elaine Harris, members of Trinity Cathedral in Portland, Oregon, are quite articulate about how they have been transformed by the spiritual practice of offering healing. Here is an excerpt from their interview.

FG: Do you feel that God's presence is more available to you personally as a result of your participation in the healing ministry?

GH: Yes, no doubt about that. It is so true. For me there is a kind of mechanical explanation in that one of the issues all of us are struggling with is getting beyond ego. The training, the practice, and all of the positive reinforcement of directing God's positive flow to other people helps me to get outside of myself and be more open, more beholden to God. This is incredibly reinforcing and very strengthening. So, yes, I am certain that I am in a stronger relationship with God in this practice of prayer and healing.

FG: How about you, Elaine?

EH: I have difficulty speaking to that question because it is so profound. I am in God's hands, and those I love are in God's hands.

Judy Sprunger is a lay member of the healing team at Westminster Presbyterian Church in Portland, Oregon, mentioned in chapter 3. In this excerpt from my interview with her, it becomes clear that she has experienced transformation because of her healing practice.

FG: Do you see anything happening in the lives of the people who have been trained?

JS: It has been an ineffable experience for all of us. We tend to feel that it is a privilege to be able to pray with people, to lay on hands, and to listen to their concerns.

FG: Yes, I know the experience.

JS: I think that it has been a growing experience for all of us. It is something that is helping me continue on the path in my walk with God. Not that I have arrived anywhere, by any means!

The Presbytery [a group of Presbyterian congregations in the area] met at our church about a year ago. We offered a healing and wholeness service after the meeting. I thought of the people coming forward for prayer and laying on of hands, some would be pastors. Before the training I would not have imagined myself laying on hands and praying for a pastor, but that service was an amazing experience. I am much more comfortable saying to someone, "Can we lay hands on you and pray?"

I was down visiting my mother, and a dear friend of hers was dying. He had had a heart attack and was not expected to live more than a day or two. My mother is a wonderful, very strong woman, but she just put her head down on the table and started crying. I simply put my arms around her and held her. Then, I found that I was spontaneously praying out loud. I probably would not have done that before my experience in the healing team.

FG: So your confidence level has risen?

JS: Oh, definitely yes.

FG: Asking the question a little differently, what value and meaning does this healing ministry have for you personally?

JS: I have been interested in healing for a long time, going back to my teens or early twenties. So having it affirmed to me that this is not something done only by the apostles, something that was available only to them. It is available to all of us, if we are open to it. To me that has been a wonderful thing.

FG: That it is available to all of us who follow Jesus?

JS: Yes, yes, and that we can all be healers. Some people may have a stronger gift of healing, but to me, it has been wonderful to know that we, too, can be healers, that God can use me, if I am open to that.

There is so much pain, so much hurt, so much sickness and grief, all around us. Being a small part of God's healing of others is something that brings me joy. Maybe that is the best way to say it. I hate to miss the healing service. I'm impoverished and poorer for not being there.

FG: Is there anything that I haven't asked you that you would like to comment on?

JS: I think it is important to be able to be together with like-minded people.

FG: The community of spirit?

JS: Yes, because I think that we help each other to grow. That is one reason why I feel impoverished when I'm not with the group. It feeds me and helps me to grow.

FG: Yes, that is an important issue, the rewards of being part of a spiritual community that is committed to healing prayer. When I'm with such a community, there is such camaraderie, a companionship in the spirit that lifts me.

JS: There is a deep feeling of community.

Baine Palmer, minister of Unity in the Valley in Eugene, Oregon, is very observant of how the healing ministry transforms individual laypeople. Below is an excerpt from my interview with him.

BP: I have been impressed with the healing and spiritual growth of the people who have gone through the training. Some of the people that we chose for the training would never have stepped forward on their own. I knew they had this gift. To see this expansion and growth is impressive. I recently wrote a letter to the healing team saying that we had another successful year. We realized that in the healing ministry the giver and the receiver complement each other. One is born out of the other. The question might be, Who is giving and who is receiving in the healing prayer process? There is something else that happens when we set up the sanctuary for the Taizé healing service. There is a spiritual energy that is created. It is a sustainable energy that goes into the consciousness of the whole church.

FG: Are laypeople being empowered as they care for one another in the healing ministry?

BP: Yes. There is a "give and take" between the healers and those who receive it. Each side receives from the other. That is a kind of empowerment, and I think that there is also a kind of empowerment happening in families. For instance, if I come to the service and receive a healing or if I come and pray for someone in my family, there is a spiritual empowerment in that and a quickening of faith. These letters that we receive indicate that there is a family empowerment of a spiritual nature. It is quiet and subtle, but it is there when you hear one person speak about another person in their family who had a healing.

Inge Tarantola is a Unity minister in Roseburg, Oregon. She observes spiritual formation among laity that goes beyond prayer and meditation. Before serving part-time at the Roseberg congregation, she was a member of Unity in the Valley in Eugene. Here is an excerpt from my interview with her.

FG: Do you see anything happening in the life of your congregation or in the lives of people who have been influenced by the healing ministry?

IT: I do. I'm glad to say that people who took training are evolving spiritually and growing in their prayer life.

FG: That is good to hear.

IT: By that I mean that we have other ways of doing prayer at Unity in the Valley and in Roseburg. I see an interest in a broader spectrum of prayer among those who took the training. For instance, we offer contemplative prayer training, and we recently added the chaplaincy program at Unity in the Valley.

I see growth in people who tell me about their spiritual journey or their daily spiritual practice. I see that in a broad sense because it includes more than prayer and meditation, but the focus is much the same. It's just that it finds a wide variety of different expressions. Prayer is a very essential part of that.

FG: Was this influenced by the healing training?

IT: Sure. This is true not only for those who trained but those who come to the healing service. Some of them make appointments to come to the Monday healing circle.

FG: Do you see spiritual growth and transformation in the people who have gone through the training and who are in the healing prayer ministry?

IT: Yes, I do. When they tell me about their ordinary life experiences, it is now from a new perspective. For instance, when they go into a job search, they have a whole different list of priorities. Earlier they might have said, "I need to support myself. What is it going to pay?" It is clear that there is a shift all around in the individuals as well as in the congregation.

FG: As a minister, watching that change must be very encouraging to see how spirit is at work.

IT: Yes, it is. Earlier you asked about the laypeople being empowered. At Unity in the Valley we've instituted one more thing: the chaplaincy program. Its primary purpose is to supplement and give relief to the ministerial team (Baine Palmer, Nola Woodbury, Sherry Lady, and Inge Tarantola), and to connect with individuals in our membership. Those in the chaplaincy program make regular monthly phone calls, simply a wellness call, a check-in: "How are you doing?" They establish a relationship through these phone calls. It creates kind of a sense of family, since we are a large congregation. Their primary phone contact is to check in with the people, offer prayer if that is requested, and offer to visit anyone who is not well. I believe that the consciousness around chaplaincy grew out of the work that you did with us.

FG: Is that right?

IT: Several of the people who have now become chaplains will offer one-on-one prayer in the sanctuary after the service for people who request it. This starts next Sunday. In part it is an outgrowth of our prayer ministry that has been in place for ten years. In part, it is a raising of consciousness through the training that we had with you four years ago. Some of the chaplains are those who received healing training. Your program has definitely had an influence in raising the consciousness and raising the level of commitment.

FG: That is good to hear.

IT: The requirements for this chaplaincy program are pretty stringent. You have to take the chaplaincy training and commit to praying with people three Sundays a month. It is a whole different level of commitment. To me it is great that people are willing to commit at that level.

FG: Yes, and that is certainly empowering the laity.

IT: Yes, and the setting in the Sunday morning service will not be nearly as private. The people will pray right then and there after the service in the sanctuary.

FG: Interesting model.

IT: Our purpose is not to get their entire story, but to get a very succinct request and then to pray with them.

FG: So you are encouraging people to ask for God's help.

IT: Exactly.

FG: That is very significant for their transformation.

IT: Yes, it is. I am hopeful, optimistic, and encouraged. It's great stuff. When I speak to them, there is something qualitatively different than attending a Sunday morning service. It is clear that something has touched them in a very unique and special way. They cherish it, in addition to coming to a Sunday morning service. I see that it touches their hearts, expands their spiritual experience in a new and different way. It also expands their understanding of spirit.

FG: Do people ever express prayer requests for something other than a personal illness?

IT: Yes, we have a lot of prayer requests for global peace. We have a lot of requests where one person will come and request prayer for another. We have a fair number of proxy healing requests where one person sits in as proxy for an individual who is ill.

FG: Were there any requests for prayer during the buildup toward war with Iraq and during the war itself?

IT: Yes, that was a great concern also.

FG: So healing was not only for individual wounds, but also healing for the globe?

IT: Yes, definitely. The area of Eugene near the university is pretty liberal. We had a lot of opposition to the war expressed.

FG: I am glad that people see healing both in the personal sense and in the global sense. The healing prayer energy for peace is the same energy as for cancer, but it takes a different form, a different kind of wound.

IT: Yes, indeed.

Inge Tarantola's ministry has been influenced by Trinity Episcopal Cathedral's Center for Spiritual Development in Portland under the leadership of Canon Marianne Borg, to whom she expresses gratitude.

There are five congregations in Oregon that now have new ministries of healing because of Canon Borg's pioneering effort in establishing a monthly healing service at Trinity Episcopal Cathedral in 1997. Through her leadership at the cathedral, Canon Borg did not set out to seed these new ministries, but in my view the Spirit used the Taizé healing services at Trinity as a magnet to draw others from near and far into new ministries where the Spirit has an opportunity to do its healing work.

If John Dominic Crossan is right about the disciples being the first people whom Jesus healed, and that they later went on to heal others, then part of their own continuing healing was precisely their empowerment to heal others. They were "a network of shared healing with Jesus."[52]

In my view, the individuals interviewed above are examples of Crossan's "healed healers." The work of the Spirit cannot be "disguised" (to use the language of Bishop Swing) in what these individuals have described. Throughout my healing ministry over the past thirty years it is clear to me that my own brokenness is healed again and again in offering healing to others.

HEALING PRACTICE INFLUENCES THE CONGREGATION

Healing prayer is a whole-making process in the life of an individual, and the same process applies in the life of a congregation. Those individuals offering prayer have an opportunity to become co-creators with God and Christ. The more people who pray for others in a congregation, the greater is the opportunity for the Spirit to shape their lives in God and to bring Christ's presence and influence into the life of that parish. Not only do individuals change, grow, and transform when they receive prayer from others in the congregation, but those offering prayer also change. A significant minority of individuals praying for one another and for the needs of the world in a congregation can change its atmosphere and make it a more caring spiritual community.

Laypeople and clergy share equally in the conduct of the ministry of healing in all the congregations described in this book. Each congregation develops its own unique style of healing practice. The clergy in all of these congregations are deeply committed to empowering the laity for their various ministries of care and healing.

Of course the clergy perform a coordinating, administrative function so that healing is integrated with other forms of pastoral care in the larger life of the parish. In these parishes pastoral care is not confined to pastors. When Steve Harms of Peace Lutheran Church wanted to introduce an experimental form of intercessory prayer for the congregation as it worships (Prayer in the Pews), he turned to members of the healing team, who understood the concept immediately and were eager to practice intercessory prayer in a new context.

When Baine Palmer at Unity in the Valley wanted to introduce a ministry of trained lay chaplains to go into the pews at the conclusion of the worship service to pray with individuals who wanted intercession, he turned to members of the healing team to implement this new form of pastoral care conducted by laity. Both Steve Harms and Baine Palmer view members of the healing team as colleagues in ministry. These forms of intercessory prayer provide the Holy Spirit a greater opportunity to influence the larger life of the congregation. In tiny, incremental steps the congregation becomes a healing community as the Spirit has deeper access to the minds and hearts of the people of God.

CHAPTER 7

Prayer Meets Science:
Cooperation, Not Conflict

The great strength of science is that it is rooted in actual experience. The great weakness of contemporary science is that it admits only certain types of experience as legitimate.[53]

—David Bohm

Harvard Medical School is a leader in building bridges of understanding between scientific medicine and spirituality through its programs of continuing education for health care professionals. Each year since the mid-1990s, the school has offered a two-day series called Spirituality & Healing in Medicine. In 2004, the course title was The Enhanced Importance of the Integration of Mind/Body Practices and Prayer.[54] The announcement says that the course provides participants with an understanding of the following:

- The role of spiritual practices in medicine and clinical care
- The scientific evidence that prayer, deep breathing, and meditation are valued therapies

- The physiologic, molecular, and neurologic effects of prayer and deep breathing
- The steps for wider incorporation of these spiritual practices into health care

The course description quotes a National Institutes for Health and Human Services report saying that in 2002, more than half of all Americans used mind/body approaches to better health. The most commonly used intervention was praying for oneself. In addition, a growing number of researchers on the faculties of medical schools at Duke, Columbia, George Washington University, University of California at San Francisco, and University of Minnesota, to name but a few, are exploring spirituality as a significant resource for the recovery from illness.

Spiritual practices can enable patients to experience transcendent meaning and to clarify or focus their life's purpose. This new way of seeing can then be integrated into the larger framework of their lives. Medical educators have become aware of the importance of including the spiritual needs and abilities of patients in their curriculum. Dr. Larry Dossey has observed that "in 1993 ... only three of the nation's 125 medical schools had courses in which the role of spirituality in healthcare was discussed. Today, around 100 medical schools have such. Though controversial in some quarters, this change is dramatic and reflects a return to medicine's historical roots."[55]

One of the earliest scientific experiments using laying on of hands—a study of the gifted healer Oskar Estebany—measured accelerated wound healing in laboratory mice. The research was conducted by Professor Bernard R. Grad and colleagues at McGill University in Montreal, Canada, in the early 1960s. Larry Dossey, MD, describes the experiment:

> Grad was the first person to study the effects of nonlocal healing intention on the healing of wounds. He anesthetized forty-eight mice and created uniform surgical incisions on their backs by removing a piece of skin about one-half by one

and a half inches. A healer held the cages of one-third of the mice for fifteen minutes twice daily while trying to heal them by mental means. One third of the mice were placed in cages that were adjusted to the same temperature as the cages being held by the healer. The remaining one-third of the mice served as controls, being moved about as the other two groups but receiving no healing intent and no additional heating. The rates of healing of the wounds of all the mice were assessed by tracing the wound shape on paper, cutting out the tracing, and weighing the cutout. After fourteen days, the treated group had healed with significantly greater rapidity than the control group, with less than one chance in a thousand that the results were due to chance.[56]

Another landmark study was conducted by San Francisco cardiologist Randolph C. Byrd, and results were published in the *Southern Medical Journal* in 1988. It was a well-designed, randomized, double-blind experiment with 393 heart patients, half of whom received prayer from a variety of church groups outside the hospital over a period of weeks. The patients in the study were randomly assigned to the treatment group or the control group. Neither the hospital staff nor the patients knew who was in which group. Those who offered prayer never met any of the patients.

The results were impressive. Patients in the test group who received prayer had fewer episodes of heart failure, cardiopulmonary arrest, and pneumonia, and less need for antibiotics and diuretics. The statistical findings showed that intercessory prayer had a positive and measurable effect on the patients who were in the test group. A flood of letters bearing heated criticism poured into the editor of the *Journal*, claiming that the article was trying to return medicine to the Dark Ages. Other correspondents strongly disagreed with the critics, suggesting that such articles were quite necessary because medicine needs objective, scientific assessment of prayer as a resource for healing.[57]

Healing Research is a comprehensive review by psychiatrist Dr. Daniel J. Benor, who surveyed the literature on scientific studies of healing.[58] He gathered reports of several hundred experimental studies describing the effects of spiritual healing on both human and nonhuman life forms. The reports describe the effects of prayer and other spiritual interventions on bacteria, cells, seeds, plants, fungi, yeast, amoebas, and animals. More than half the experiments showed that spiritual interventions were effective. Such interventions promoted health or growth, cured or prevented sickness, or prevented the death of the organism. Dr. Benor observed that skeptics who sought to demolish claims for spiritual healing had great difficulty explaining away the results of these nonhuman studies, which have been replicated again and again.

Ours is a culture in which science and spirituality have been radically separated for hundreds of years and have often existed in opposition. This has led us to experience the self as isolated from everyone and everything else, in a delusion of separateness that is our ordinary consciousness.

We each have individual thoughts and feelings, plans and destinies, talents and desires. But, human nature is also amphibious. Part of it swims in the water of the cosmic realm where one becomes aware that one is not separate but part of the whole. Part of it walks on the dry land of our unique individuality.

At the level of ultimate reality, no individual is separate from the billions of other people on the planet today. Quantum physicists insist that each person is an integral part of the whole universe. Dr. Dossey describes this paradox: "Although we seem to be different individuals inhabiting separate bodies, we are intimately connected with each other at some level of the mind. This image has surfaced consistently throughout human history. It permeates the language of poets, artists, and mystics, and has been repeatedly understood by spiritual adepts in all the great religious traditions."[59]

Thus, in addition to being individuals with our own specific paths and destinies, we are also deeply interconnected with one another. If the delusion of separation at the level of our ultimate interconnectedness can be removed, then it is possible to have a radically changed perception of human nature. We can see that the human being is not a separate person isolated from other separate people and that human nature is both individual and cosmically intertwined at the same time.

It is very difficult for the modern, commonsense mind to wrap itself around the fact that this sense of separateness could be thought of as a delusion of consciousness. Insights from quantum physics reveal, however, that not only are we *not* separated from one another, but we are also *not* separated from the whole. Science writer Gary Zukav has observed the following:

> Quantum mechanics shows us that we are not separate from the rest of the world as we once thought. Particle physics shows us that the "rest of the world" does not sit idly "out there." It is a sparkling realm of continual creation, transformation, and annihilation. The ideas of the new physics, when wholly grasped, can produce extraordinary *experience*. The study of relativity theory, for example, can produce the remarkable experience that space and time are only mental constructions. Each of these different experiences is capable of changing us in such ways that we never again are able to view the world as we did before.[60]

Physician Mike Denney sees quantum physics as the peculiar new science that insists that reality is discontinuous and paradoxical. Quantum reality does not follow the rules of cause-and-effect common sense or empirical science as we know it in a Newtonian worldview. Denney describes how physicist Max Planck introduced the notion of *quanta* as a mathematical formula that was written on a postcard to his friend Heinrich Ruben in 1900. Quanta are tiny, discrete bundles of energy that act like both waves and particles. Applying the principles of quantum physics gave us CAT scans, transistors, and lasers. However, it is difficult to see everyday events in our lives as quantum phenomena.

Is intercessory prayer at a distance a form of focused consciousness that can change reality? Yes, that has been my experience. Can healing prayer at a distance be understood by using quantum mechanics as a framework for reality? Perhaps. Dr. Denney quotes Amit Goswamy, a theoretical physicist from the University of Oregon: "A quantum object cannot be said to manifest in ordinary space-time reality until we observe it as a particle."[61] In physics, this focus of consciousness is called the "observer effect," which means that we can change reality just by looking at it. Does quantum theory suggest "that an observation that collapses a wave into a particle [has] anything to do with human goals, desires, or will upon the cells of the body"? Dr. Denney is not certain what the answer is, because that hypothesis uses linear, cause-and-effect reasoning that does not apply to nonlinear, quantum phenomena that are outside of time and space categories.

> Yet some of us—including medical doctors—believe that the principles of quantum physics are an essential component of all healing. We point out that although modern medicine claims to be scientific, it operates with an empirical science that is based upon seventeenth-century, Newtonian cause-and-effect, mechanical physics, and the Cartesian split of mind and body. In this spirit of Positivism [sense perceptions are the only admissible basis of human knowledge], both the modern standards of medical care and the laws of our culture demand that the treatment of illness, whether conventional, alternative, complementary, or spiritual, must be supported with the hard evidence derived by classical science's statistical, clinical studies that prove or disprove the effectiveness of any modality. As a result, the dramatic quantum discoveries of the twentieth century have not yet been included in

the practices of the medical healing arts. There are those of us who envision a change in consciousness, a paradigm shift, which would include quantum phenomena into the healing of mind and body.[62]

HOW DID MODERN MEDICINE EVOLVE TO INCLUDE SPIRITUALITY?

In his book *Reinventing Medicine,* Larry Dossey divides the history of medicine in the United States since the Civil War into three eras. Dossey sees Era I *as* Mechanical Medicine, bringing the scientific method into medicine. This "encompasses the therapies that largely dominate Western medicine today—drugs, surgery, radiation, and so on. The entire universe is viewed as clockwork and functions according to cause and effect. Matter and energy are important, not mind."[63]

He describes Era II as Mind-Body Medicine that developed after World War II and grew out of research in the field of psychosomatic disease. In ancient Greece, physicians were aware of how emotions influenced our physical health, and they explored the place of dreams in healing.

Dossey observed that after World War I there began to be an awareness that the mind could affect the body, as thousands of soldiers returned home with "shell shock," the disease we now know as post-traumatic stress disorder, or PTSD.

However, physicians in Era II medicine were trained to equate the mind with the brain. He notes, "Era II or 'mind-body' medicine is often constrained by the purely physical 'brain-body' medicine of Era I."[64]

Era III is described as Nonlocal Medicine, which "does not confine or localize the mind to the brain and body. It grants the mind freedom to roam freely in space and time."[65]

Drawing on a view of reality influenced by this new physics, Dossey and others suggest that part of our mind is not present in our body or brain or even participating in this present moment, but is outside of time, "spread everywhere, extending billions of miles into space, from the beginnings of time into the limitless future, linking us with the minds of one another and with everyone who has ever lived or will live. This is the infinite piece of your consciousness."[66]

Viewed from the perspective of my Christian tradition, this "nonlocal" awareness is a description of the human soul, which is individual and, at the same time, part of the divine cosmos. This dual and paradoxical quality of human nature is beautifully expressed in this prayer by J. Philip Newell:

> Bless to me O God
> My soul that comes from on high.
> Bless to me O God
> My body that is of earth.[67]

The human being can be understood as both soul and body, capable of inhabiting both heaven and earth. Simultaneously, at our highest level of functioning, we seek to integrate the two realms, the heavenly and the earthly. In Dossey's language, the individual mind is part of the larger universal mind. In my Christian language, I understand the individual soul is part of the mind of God and connected to all other souls.

Dossey points out that the "medical implications of this are profound."[68] As we are part of the whole *(and the holy)* the nature of our being allows us to help heal one another through and in the wholeness of God, as we are part and parcel of the wholeness of God. If *we are one body*, then both our illnesses as well as our prayers are collective. When I am asked to lead a healing, I am entering into the consciousness of God (or more correctly I become aware of God consciousness, as I can never be separated from the Holy). God is continually breathing into my very spirit and body as I am breathing into God. We can come into union in the healing prayer, caring for one another at a level of depth that is comforting for both the one being healed and the healer. Dossey says, "When illness occurs, the fact that I can help you and you can help me eases the isolation and feelings of being alone that are a painful part of being sick."[69] An ill person who comes to a healing service or prayer group in a congregation is not alone; he or she feels cared for and loved. That supporting love is an important and integral part of the healing.

HOW DO WE EXPAND OUR HEALING CONSCIOUSNESS?

It seems to me that God is constantly seeking to love us into a higher level of spiritual maturity, wanting us to become more conscious of our God-self, or soul, and conscious of all other souls. In the poetic lines of Psalm 139 is a beautiful image of God seeking us:

> O Lord, you have searched me and known me
> You know when I sit down and when I rise up;
> you discern my thoughts from far away.
> You search out my path and my lying down,
> and are acquainted with all my ways.
> Where can I go from your spirit?
> or where can I flee from your presence?
> (Psalm 139:1–3 and 7)

In my edition of the Bible the words *The Inescapable God* provide a descriptive title for the Psalm and appear just above verse 1. Our human pursuit of the Holy is thus a double search. We pursue God, and simultaneously the inescapable God searches us out. Implied in the Psalm is the assumption that there is no place in the universe where God is not present. Psalm 139 could rightly be described as a nonlocal view of God, to use Dossey's term drawn from quantum physics. God cannot be confined to any particular place or any particular time. This means that God is simultaneously local and nonlocal.

That is the paradox. If we are indeed linked to one another and at the same time linked to the universe or God, then an intercessory prayer by one person for the healing of another at a distance makes a good deal of sense. Each of us is already connected to every other person on the planet, but if we are unaware of the potential for healing that this reality represents, we get trapped in that delusion of consciousness referred to earlier, in which we believe we are separate from one another.

Prayer for another person is a form of focused consciousness. If the universe is a single organism and each of us is already connected to every person in the universe, then focused prayer for another is a way of recognizing and acknowledging that existing connection. The prayer for healing focuses our attention, our consciousness, and brings that already-present connection into awareness as we widen our circle and feel at one with that person, with God's creation, and with God.

In an interview in the journal *Alternative Therapies in Health and Medicine*, Dr. Dossey was asked if he had any idea why intercessory prayer works. In responding, he said, "A major question is whether prayer works because of some specific, direct impact of consciousness, or because of some transempirical factors." He went on to ask a rhetorical question: "Does your intention—whether we call that a prayer, a wish, or something else—tweak the universe? Or does the Absolute, however named, intervene and create the effect?"[70]

In considering those questions myself, I began to think about a third way of posing the issue, based on thirty years of teaching a method of healing that was fashioned by Lawrence LeShan, with whom I had studied. It deals with the illusion of separateness. When one prays for a subject, one moves from inside-a-shell consciousness into an experience of transcendental consciousness. One becomes unified with the Absolute and at the same time invites the ill person into that experience of union. Before the act of praying, one feels a sense of separation that is a natural part of ordinary consciousness. In the act of praying or focusing one's intentionality, one moves out of the delusion of separateness into an experience of unity, grounded in the One.

In my view, prayer tears down the prison walls of little-ego consciousness. With the walls down, God has an opportunity to flood in to do God's whole-making, healing work. God has been there all along, waiting for us to become aware of our walls and recognize our prison.

LeShan observed that "Prayer attempts to mobilize the energies of the One for another."[71] Prayer tears down the illusory walls of separation and opens both the subject and the healer to the energies of the One, so that in oneness the healing can happen. It is more an allowing, a relaxing, letting go into being rather than *doing* anything.

Julian of Norwich, a fourteenth-century English mystic, said that "Prayer *ones* the soul to God." She enjoys turning the noun *one* into a verb. In another place: "We were all created at the same time, and in our creation we were knit and *oned* to God... God never began to love us ... we have always been ... known and loved from without beginning."[72] Julian had a nonlocal view of time. On reading these lines from Julian, a physicist who participated in one of my healing retreats said that Julian was six hundred years ahead of her day because she articulated a perception of time that could easily have been stated by a quantum physicist in the twentieth century.

When still a young woman, Julian became very ill. As she lay dying, a priest was called to administer last rites. As he held a crucifix before her, she prayed to Christ and offered up her life to God. "And suddenly in that moment all my pain left me, and I was as sound ... as ever I was before or have been since. I was astonished by this change, for it seemed to me that it was by God's secret doing and not natural."[73]

Using Dossey's language, what one might call the nonlocal Christ came to Julian in a vision as she surrendered her life to God. She was physically healed in the process of praying, becoming one with God through her connecting prayer to Christ. Christ appeared to her and spoke to her. She later wrote down Christ's words in *Book of Showings*. Her prayer dissolved the "delusion" of separateness. In the process, she was healed and made whole, by God's grace that manifested in her vision of Christ.

In Dossey's language, the infinite part of her consciousness, her nonlocal mind, ventured outside the present and beyond measurable space. Dr. Dossey observes that "this part of your mind can be used today in healing illness and disease in what I call Era III healing."[74]

Is not such a mystical experience illustrative of the fact that a human being is a part of the whole? The vision is a mechanism of communication or linkage between the part and the whole, between the soul and the Whole, or God.

WHAT DOES LOVE HAVE TO DO WITH HEALING?

The delusion of separateness helps to keep us in a prison of self-absorption. To free ourselves from this prison, we are called to love, by widening our circle of compassion to embrace all living creatures. This brings us to the question, What does love have to do with healing? Can love bridge the gap caused by separateness and isolation? Can it help to dissolve the delusion that we are separate?

A study at Stanford Medical School showed that women participating in a breast cancer support group lived an average of eighteen months longer than those who received only traditional medical treatment. These studies demonstrate that loving support, many social ties, and close relationships are important factors in maintaining health. Loving support helps to release us from the prison of separateness.[75]

Three psychiatrists (Thomas Lewis, Fari Amini, and Richard Lannon) who formerly taught at the University of California Medical School in San Francisco speak to this in a watershed book, *A General Theory of Love*:

> The first half of the twentieth century brought dazzling technologies—antibiotics, vaccines, X rays, anesthesia—that delivered sophisticated diagnostic acumen and unparalleled ability to cure. The age ushered in was also one of estrangement from patients. For the last thirty years the paradox of Western medicine has been the seemingly inexplicable coexistence of technical excellence with unpopularity. Americans receive the world's most advanced treatments, biochemical miracles in power and scope. Yet patients complain fiercely.

Doctors don't listen, patients say; they are cold and busy technocrats. And the patients are right, because American medicine has come to rely on intellect as the agency of cure … [Patients] want someone who connects with them in spite of their suffering; they wish for a warm hand on their shoulder and the security of speaking with someone who has been through this before.[76]

So it seems we are yearning for a true and genuine connection with one another and that this union in and of itself can be healing. I often see an intuitive awareness of connection operating during the five-day healing retreats I conduct several times a year, where it is common for participants to enter deeply altered states of consciousness. In these retreats, I teach people to offer healing prayer that is grounded in God's love. The students practice contemplative exercises and pray together over a period of several days, not only using words but in silent contemplative exercises as well.

During the retreat, a profound resonance develops among participants, and they seem to move into a deep connectedness with one another. A profound spiritual coherence often develops by the third or fourth day. The contemplative and meditation exercises stimulate the brain to function in a way that it hasn't since very early childhood.

During a retreat some years ago, I remember praying as part of a healing group with a woman participant, bringing as much of God's love to her as I could imagine. In some of our exercises and prayer circles, images come onto the screen of consciousness, and we check to see what meaning they might have. One of the images that spontaneously came into my mind's eye when praying for this woman was a B-17 bomber flying on a mission over Germany during World War II. I was astonished and asked myself, "What can that military image possibly have to do with my healing prayer with this woman?"

During the sharing period, I almost did not mention that image because I felt too embarrassed, but I finally decided to speak up despite my discomfort. At the conclusion of the sharing, the woman commented on several of the images offered by participants. She then turned to me and said, "My husband flew B-17 bombers over Germany during World War II." I was dumbfounded. It seems to me that my consciousness had somehow connected to her consciousness in my prayer for her highest good. Momentarily, it seemed that the delusion of separateness had disappeared.

Is it possible that we had experienced a heart-to-heart connection at a nonlocal level during this prayer?

During these retreats, connections happen to many people during our deep contemplative prayers for healing. In praying for others, a bond is made from one heart to another and to the Holy as we ask God's love to move through us. This action releases us from our prison—our delusion of separateness—and also provides a deep heart connection to God and Christ and to the person with whom we pray. As Julian of Norwich observed, "Prayer ones the soul to God."

These heart-to-heart phenomena are signs that we are all connected—"wired" to one another, so to speak—in a nonlocal, quantum explanation of reality. In those moments, the delusion of separateness can at times dissolve. We are not only "part of the whole" but part of one another. Intercessory prayer not only "ones the soul to God" but also lovingly bonds the soul of the one praying to the soul of the person who is ill. If each of us is part of the whole, then we are, and always have been, connected to the person with whom we are praying. The loving prayer brings that linkage into consciousness and builds a healing connection to God and to the ill person simultaneously.

Love is the heart-to-heart-to-God connection. Love is the energy and quality of intention that seeks to reduce the distance and erode the separateness that damages our relationship to ourselves, our neighbor, our world, and the creator God.

CAN THESE GIFTS BE MISUSED?

In chapter 12 of his first letter to the Corinthians, the apostle Paul warns them about the misuse of spiritual gifts.

> Now there are varieties of gifts, but the same Spirit; and there are varieties of services, but the same Lord; and there are varieties of activities, but it is the same God that activates all of them in everyone. To each is given the manifestation of the Spirit for the common good. To one is given through the Spirit the utterance of wisdom, and to another the utterance of knowledge according to the same Spirit, to another faith by the same Spirit, to another gifts of healing by the one Spirit, to another the working of miracles, to another prophecy, to another the discernment of spirits, to another various kinds of tongues, to another the interpretation of tongues. (1 Corinthians 12:4–10)

Paul goes on to explain the spiritual hazards that sometimes emerge in the use of these wonderful gifts. Chapter 13 begins with a warning disclaimer about how to interpret these spiritual gifts. He makes it very clear that the gifts have no validity at all unless they are grounded in love.

> If I speak in the tongues of mortals and of angels, but do not have love, I am a noisy gong or a clanging cymbal. And if I have prophetic powers, and understand all mysteries and all knowledge, and if I have all faith so as to remove mountains, but do not have love, I am nothing. If I give away all of my possessions, and if I hand over my body so that I may boast, but do not have love, I gain nothing. (I Corinthians 13:1–3)

These chapters should not be read individually but as a single unit, as it was in the original Greek manuscripts. Paul especially emphasized his warning in chapter 13 that spiritual gifts exercised without love are a fraud, "a noisy gong or a clanging symbol," and for good reason. If the gifts are not validated by love, then the person with the gifts gains nothing. When this magnificent hymn of love is read in public, it is seldom set in the context of a love that guides the use of spiritual gifts. Healing is a spiritual gift, and like the other gifts, its motivation needs to be validated by love so that the little ego does not become inflated. Like all other gifts, healing can be distorted if the little ego becomes attached to the dramatic healing results that sometimes occur. I caution my students that the spontaneous intuition that often happens in the training retreats can also become a phenomenon to which the little ego becomes attached.

Love knows at the very deepest level that each of us is part of the whole, that each of us is part of the other, that we are each "wired" to one another, though our commonsense perception says otherwise. Love has a wisdom that is patient and kind. It seeks always to reduce the distance, close the separateness gap between one human and another.

Life magazine published an article some years ago titled "The Rescuing Hug," which included a photograph of twins born twelve weeks prematurely. After birth, they were whisked into their separate incubators. One of the twins had breathing and heart-rate problems and failed to gain weight. She was not expected to live. A hospital nurse fought against the hospital rules and placed the babies in one incubator. When they were placed together, the healthier of the two threw an arm over her sister in an endearing embrace. The smaller baby's heart rate stabilized and her temperature rose to normal. They both survived and are thriving. Continued separateness would quite likely have brought death to the weaker twin.[77]

Love heals. When we pray for another person's health, we are inviting God's love and expressing our love. According to Agnes Sanford, the great healer and teacher of healing, "Only love can generate the healing fire … when we pray in accordance with the will of God."[78]

Science and spirituality no longer need to live in opposition to each other. This three-hundred-year conflict is a conflict of human belief systems. Science and spirituality need to hold each other in love. The insights of quantum physics help us to understand that the clash is a false duality imposed out of a Newtonian worldview that has no valid way to evaluate distant-healing prayer or visionary experiences. These experiences illustrate Einstein's assertion that a human being is part of the whole (see chapter 8). Sir Isaac Newton's worldview supports and promotes the delusion that each of us is something separate.

To my mind, there is no easier way to widen our circle of compassion than by offering healing prayer with others that expresses God's love and follows the example set by Jesus. It is no accident that a very significant part of Jesus's ministry, and that of the disciples whom he sent out, was committed to God's love expressed in healing. As followers of Jesus in our generation, it seems to me that we, too, are sent out to express God's compassion to those in pain. He taught his disciples how to heal, and they passed on that capability, that confidence, and that gift to succeeding generations. By God's grace, these have now come down to our generation, which is strongly conditioned by the scientific worldview. This chapter suggests that it is possible to deepen our understanding of healing within that scientific framework. Jesus began his healing with the original twelve disciples; all we need to do is accept the reality of his gift and continue to practice the divine healing that he began.

CHAPTER 8

Healing Is the Practice of Compassion

Prayer for others opens a space in which we become conscious of an unconditional loving presence. Intercessory prayer creates a sacred space to which we all belong, so that we enter a community held in God, framed by God, as well as finding God present to each of us directly in unmediated presence.[79]

—Ann Belford Ulanov

Healing has been part of the human struggle to hold illness at bay since the dawn of time. Evidence of this is found in 15,000-year-old cave drawings in France that illustrate the use of hands for healing. Congregations in the church's first generation practiced a form of healing prayer and laying on of hands that the apostles must have learned from Jesus. Not only did he give them authority to heal, but it is quite likely that he gave them specific instructions about how to heal as well. People in those first-century congregations cared deeply about one another, and for that reason they can be called compassionate communities.

Healing is an opportunity to practice compassion within community. The congregation that takes prayer for others seriously provides the Spirit with a way to renew the church. In this practice, the Spirit is given access to the hearts of its people to do God's work.

That is where any renewal must begin. It is the Spirit that stimulates the work of renewal. It does not originate in our human genius or creative planning. Prayer for healing and laying on of hands is one practice that enables a congregation to take prayer seriously and become open to the Spirit. Over time people discover that prayer can, by God's grace, make a difference in releasing the shackles of pain and accelerating the speed of recovery from illness. Healing prayer is grounded in love that makes a person more whole in love's Holy presence.

Many people in mainline Protestant congregations today feel an inarticulate longing for wholeness and healing as they seek to deal with the burdens and pressures of living in our speeded-up world. In painful times of personal crisis, this longing is deepened. Illness comes unexpected and unannounced. Others are heartbroken or in despair or suffering grief. Through their counseling, preaching, and teaching, modern pastors respond to these burdens as best they can, drawing on the training that they have had.

Jesus commissioned his followers to take the good news of God out into the world. The Canadian Anglican priest Tom Harpur points out, "That whereas Christ told his would-be followers to preach, teach and heal, most of my efforts seemed to be concentrated on the first two (both verbal). My denomination was placing little or no emphasis on the command to offer healing of body and soul; that is, of the complete person. Certainly my training in seminary had given me no preparation whatever in this field."[80] That certainly was the case in my own seminary experience, and that of most pastors of my acquaintance.

In the United States today, healing prayer, anointing with oil, and laying on of hands are not much in evidence in most mainline congregations. It is possible for most of these congregations to become more compassionate if they set about recovering the practice that Jesus introduced so long ago.

RECEIVING HEALING PRAYER

In the fall of 1997, Trinity Episcopal Cathedral in Portland, Oregon, began to offer a Sunday evening healing service held monthly that incorporated Taizé chants, silence, readings, anointing, prayer for healing, and laying on of hands. The service was created by Canon Marianne Wells Borg of the cathedral staff. The response from the larger community was strong, and within a year attendance at the Taizé healing service was more than a hundred people each month. Within three years a Presbyterian and a Unity congregation in Oregon were inspired to create similar Taizé healing services as well. I trained the healing teams in each of these congregations. As preparation for the service the teams meet in healing prayer groups a day or so before the evening service. Individuals in need of healing have the opportunity to come to these healing prayer groups or to the service itself.

Here is a letter of thanks from a member of Unity in the Valley in Eugene, Oregon. She received prayer in a healing group. The letter was addressed to the Reverend Inge Tarantola, a member of the healing team.

Dear Inge,

In the early weeks of 2003, I had several glaucoma surgeries—with the possibility of more—and was needing support and comfort. I had read about Taizé healing services in both the Unity newsletters and Sunday programs, and they sounded promising—a little mysterious perhaps—but I couldn't imagine myself at the center of even a small group's concern. I would be embarrassed. … Maybe I could learn to be a Taizé HEALER, I thought. Certainly I would be more comfortable in that role. Since that night I have struggled to understand what I felt among the Taizé practitioners who enfolded me in their prayers and soft energy: I think I would call it a tribal experience. It was as though my tribe—some of whom I'd never met but were suddenly friends—had gathered around me and was passing its collective strength into my flagging body and spirit. I began to relax, to let myself float, buoyed by our connectedness. I forgot to be embarrassed. One moment I'd think, Oh, oh, is it over? Are they getting tired? Then I'd float again, feel the warm presence of my tribe. Near the end, someone cupped my head in his hands and spoke. His words poured out toward the universe where I felt they were heard.

I did not have another glaucoma surgery after that evening. Now, months later and with a different eye surgery scheduled, I am drawing on the confidence that remains from the hands-on healing. It's reassuring to know that I am welcome to repeat the treatment if necessary. Such an opportunity to experience the collective power of a tribe. My thanks.

Warmly, Judy

Judy experienced what many people feel who ask for healing: doubt, vulnerability, anxiety, uncertainty, and feeling terribly self-conscious. Her description of the welcoming love, sense of relaxation, and the Spirit's mysterious movement in her awareness are beautifully articulated. The origin of the healing that she describes so clearly can be traced historically to the healing practice that Jesus taught his followers.

Her congregation can certainly be characterized as a compassionate community. Judy's letter is an authentic description of God's love experienced by a person receiving healing prayer. It is obvious that people in this congregation care deeply about one another, as did members of congregations in the first century. Doubtless the specific techniques of the healing practices were somewhat different from those in today's church, but the compassionate caring expressed in the community's healing prayers was the same. God's grace and love was and is the same.

In my view the most important part of Judy's story is that in receiving prayer and laying on of hands she felt God's encompassing love flowing to her from the group's prayers. For Judy, it was a raw experience of the Holy. Her doubts and misgivings vanished. She knew she was welcome to return for another healing so that she might again experience the "collective power of a tribe," a compassionate community. A congregation becomes more compassionate the more opportunities there are to make a God connection by asking for prayers of healing and support. Every such prayer gives the Spirit an opportunity to do its holy work.

Judy imagined that someday she, too, might offer healing prayer as well as receive it. She was surprised by her experience of God in the healing group. Sometimes the healer is also surprised by what transpires in offering healing prayer.

Hospital Chaplain Surprised by Healing

It was two o'clock one morning when the Reverend Patricia Swanson Megregian was awakened by a phone call from the intensive care unit at Children's Hospital in Buffalo, New York, where she is chaplain.[81] Would she come into the hospital to offer prayer for a dying teenager? He suffered complications from surgery that filled his body with infection. His organs were shutting down, and the physicians had given him only a couple of hours longer to live. At his bedside, the mother told the chaplain that she believed that he could survive by some miracle. Chaplain Megregian describes the situation:

"I sat with her for a while talking softly about his life, about his dreams … In the intimacy of the moment, I asked her if she wanted to pray together. She said, "Yes, please." I placed one hand on the child's forehead; the other was holding his hand. I recalled the ancient tradition of the laying on of hands for the sick and dying as I closed my eyes to pray. Ordinarily, I would have begun my prayer that God be present in this difficult time for the child and for the mother, even though I knew at the same time that Mom would be praying for a miracle cure.

"But that night, in the quiet of the humming machines and the shadows of the late night deathwatch, I was led to pray something entirely different. I prayed that God's golden light of love [would] come into the child and literally push the infection out of his body. I asked for him to be completely filled with God. Suddenly, I felt my hands grow warm. They started to tingle. I felt as if I were a vessel being filled with God's love and pouring that love into this child. I was awed, frightened, and curious about this strange experience."

Chaplain Megregian looked at the mother to see how this prayer might affect her. She wondered if the mother sensed anything different from the usual prayers offered by clergy at the bedside. She ended the prayer by asking God to do what was very best for this boy. Mother and chaplain would both wait and listen for the answer. She walked out of the room and slumped against the wall. The nurse was concerned about the chaplain and asked if she was all right.

"'Yes,' I said. 'Something strange happened in there though. I'm not sure what it was, but I just laid hands on that boy and prayed for him to be healed even though I have been told he is going to die soon.

"'Listen,' I stuttered, 'something happened to my hands when I was praying. I felt a great power come through me.'

"'Jeez!' she [the nurse] said. 'You're scaring me. I've got goose bumps on my arms.'

"'Look,' I whispered, 'it could be nothing, so don't say anything to anyone. But I know something happened in there. Two hours went by and the boy was still the same. I asked the nurse to call me when there was a change.

"I never got called. I went in the next morning to find that he had pulled through the night against all odds and it looked like they were beginning to win the battle with the infection. One month later, he was getting ready to leave the hospital to go for rehabilitation, and I stopped by to say good-bye.

"'You know,' I said, 'you are my miracle boy.' He smiled at me with tears in his eyes.

"'I know. Thank you so much. Will you pray with me before I leave?'

"And we did. In this experience it all came together. I prayed with the intention of great love for that child. We connected with the power of the Holy, and the outcome was a healing of his body. The outcome could have been different. Yet it would not have negated the experience or the connection."

In that situation she offered a prayer that was out of the ordinary for her. She was influenced by the content of what she thought the mother's prayer would be—that is, asking for a miracle. The chaplain wanted to support the mother's prayer, and she was led to reach back into her own Christian tradition to lay on hands as she prayed. The mother's faith and love influenced the chaplain's prayer response, and the child was cured by the grace of God. That gift of grace is available in every moment of life, in every breath taken. This kind of healing does not happen very often, but it is real and actually does happen in today's world.

HEALED BY LOVE

Love is the root energy hidden in all creation. In human brokenness, individuals are recreated and healed by love. Prayer for healing enables the person praying to access that root energy of divine love for another person as a way of enabling God's grace and wholeness. The dying teenager began to recover as Chaplain Megregian and the mother prayed with him. When the chaplain laid on hands and prayed, the grace of God went into high gear. This transforming prayer, grounded in love, is shrouded in mystery. It can be directed toward another person in pain, or it can address one's own deepest need. The surprising power of such prayer is difficult for many believing people in this modern world to accept. They believe, but they also need help in their unbelief. These two dramatic healings are unusual. Much of the time there are no apparent results that can be measured or reported. However, that does not mean that nothing has happened. The person receiving the prayer is always more whole. Every human being alive on the planet today has the innate capacity to be an instrument of healing, to become a conduit of the Holy, to have access to the unconditional loving presence that undergirds the universe.

Mother and chaplain became one with the boy in God, and any sense of separateness fell away. In their prayer, love prompted each of them to let go of the little-ego self, and the chaplain asked that the boy be filled with God's "golden light of love." That happened, but the chaplain also became filled at the same moment. The love-saturated prayers of the mother and the chaplain enabled the boy to recover through a graced transformation of his body/mind/spirit. The chaplain served in a hospital and represented the church as compassionate community. In her chaplaincy work before this dramatic healing, she enabled God's healing grace in many forms, but the healing of the dying teenager was a new form of intercessory prayer that she was led to offer. As followers of Jesus, all of us in the church are latent healers, but we are unaware of that and don't know it unless we give God an opportunity to use us.

WE ARE ALL HEALERS

We all belong, we all live in a sacred space, and all of us have the capacity to open up that sacred space to another person who is broken, out of balance, or in pain. Intercessory prayer is a beautiful and awesome practice. However, not many people in our culture today accept that we have this capacity, even in mainline churches. To be able to open up a sacred space to another is a humbling experience, because one knows that something more powerful is at work: a grace, a gift from the Holy. One knows that one is not the source of the healing but rather a conduit carrying what might be called, in nontraditional language, a holy energy from a transcendent reality. Every person alive today has the capacity to become a healer and a conduit of the Holy.

My metaphor for healing prayer in our lives is a large field of dry grass under the light of a hot sun. Every blade of dry grass is warmed equally by the sun. However, if you hold a magnifying glass over a dry clump of grass at just the right angle, it can focus and concentrate the rays and heat of the sun to a single point, and the grass will burst into flame. If God is the sun shining equally on the entire field, then our prayers can act as a focusing lens to concentrate the light of God's love where we pray that it will go. The focused light of God's love does not always bring about a cure that can be measured, but it can still warm and heal in unexpected ways. There is no intervention by God, no favoritism, no singling out the chosen who are receiving prayer in contrast to those who are not. The warmth of God's loving light falls on every person, every blade of grass, equally. The loving heart, focused in prayer, can become a focusing lens for the healing light of God. In this metaphor, the healers can put themselves in alignment with God's light, interceding with God and focusing that light for the transformation of those who suffer.

In this model, God's healing light falls equally on everyone, but prayers of intercession are like a focusing lens for God's healing light that is directed toward a particular person. This model is in contrast to a commonly accepted concept of divine intervention, where God chooses some people in pain to receive healing and ignores others. I do not believe in a God who plays favorites. Jesus taught that God loves us all equally. "God causes the sun to rise on both the bad and the good, and sends rain on both the just and the unjust" (Matthew 5:45).[82]

Anyone can learn to become a focusing lens for the healing light, the loving force of God. We do not have to be specially gifted. Learning the art of effective healing prayer is like learning how to play the piano. To play a musical instrument one first has to be motivated, second, be willing to take regular lessons from a teacher, and third, practice every day.

This lack of awareness about our capacity to be a conduit of healing is part of our culture's belief system that persuades so many of us that although intercessory prayer for healing can't hurt anyone, it is not really effective and does not make sense. For many modern people it seems highly presumptuous for anyone to claim that she or he can, through prayer, participate in God's mysterious, holy energy for healing.

A HUMAN BEING IS PART OF THE WHOLE

Many years ago, a rabbi had two teenage daughters. One child died, and he was grieving her death while at the same time seeking to console the other daughter in her time of devastation. In his anguish, he turned to Albert Einstein, asking him in a letter what he could say to his other daughter who was in such pain. Einstein replied as follows:

> A human being is part of the whole, called by us the "Universe," a part limited in time and space. He experiences himself, his thoughts and feelings as something separated from the rest—a kind of optical delusion of his consciousness. This delusion is a kind of prison for us, restricting us to our personal desires and affection for a few persons nearest to us. Our task must be to free ourselves from this prison by widening our circle of compassion to embrace all living creatures and the whole of nature in its beauty. Nobody is able to achieve this completely, but the striving for such achievement is in itself part of the liberation and a foundation for inner security.[83]

How does healing happen? One of my mentors in healing, Lawrence LeShan, offers an interesting image. He suggests that healing happens through the healer "being part of the whole and so perception of other parts through the whole [is what heals], and *Prayer* attempts to mobilize the energies of the One for another part of it."

In my view, prayer not only "mobilizes the energies of the One"[84] but also tears down the illusory walls of separation. Prayer bonds the person in pain and the healer together as they are taken into the realm of the Holy, what LeShan calls the "One," so that healing can happen. It is more an allowing, a relaxing into *being* than it is *doing* anything. The reference here is to silent, contemplative prayer.

The healing method taught during the first two days of the five-day training retreat is grounded in about ten contemplative exercises.

What is contemplation? Contemplation is simply being present to what is, with nothing shut out, nothing excluded. Contemplation allows us to become focused and centered in the present moment, experiencing the "eternal now." In the words of St. Teresa of Avila, "The Presence, whom the soul has at its side, makes it attentive to everything."[85] These contemplative prayer exercises enable the healer, by God's grace, to be totally present to the subject who is in pain. Hence, the title of this book is *Contemplative Healing.*

When I experience healing prayer for another, it sometimes feels like an intervention, but in my view it is not. Rather it is an outward sign of a deeper awareness of my being … a letting go, a relaxing into the Holy, becoming one with all Creation and the person receiving my prayer. The fourteenth-century English mystic Julian of Norwich describes it beautifully.

> Our soul is oned to God,
> unchangeable goodness,
> and therefore
> between God and our soul
> there is neither wrath nor forgiveness
> because
> there is no between.[86]

How does sacred healing happen? It begins with love. In my view the one offering healing prayer lets go of the "little ego" and invites the person in pain to be a companion, and together they become conscious of an unconditional loving presence that we call God. In this state of awareness, there is no delusion of separateness. This process of becoming "one" with the unconditional, loving presence and becoming "one" with the person in pain is transformative. It does not explain the enormous mystery of healing, but it does offer an effective model of a way of praying that can enable God's grace for healing.

When offering prayers for healing, I ask Jesus to be present at the center of the healing. This is similar to praying in Jesus's name that was done in first-century congregations two thousand years ago. Healing practiced in the church today is a continuation of that tradition, but the practice itself has been greatly modified over the centuries. However, it is in essence what Jesus introduced to his followers. In chapter 3 there is a description of how Jesus taught his followers to offer healing.

DOES INTERCESSORY PRAYER MAKE SENSE?

On the face of it, what we call intercessory prayer for healing simply does not make sense in our culture's belief system today. How can one person's prayer stimulate the healing process in another person, sometimes miles away? Measured by the yardstick of today's common sense, healing prayer boggles the mind, yet many times I have witnessed God's grace stimulating a recovery. Reports of accelerated rates of recovery through prayer, or what some researchers call "distant healing," are beginning to appear in medical journals with increasing frequency. More and more health-care professionals are opening up to the possibility that prayer for healing might well be an effective *medical* resource for a person who is ill. In technologically developed countries, many people have no difficulty accepting healing prayer as a *spiritual* resource but find difficulty accepting it as an effective *medical* resource. Yet an increasing number of medical studies in peer-reviewed journals present evidence for the effectiveness of healing prayer.

In our culture, there is strong resistance to the claim that focused intentionality at a distance—or in religious language, intercessory prayer—is effective and can be supported scientifically. In his book *Reinventing Medicine,* Larry Dossey, MD, describes a number of scientific studies of distant healing conducted over the last two decades:[87]

"Leonard Laskow, an American gynecologist and healer, was able to inhibit the growth rate of cancer cells, as measured by their uptake of radioactive thymidine, a standard index of DNA synthesis, using appropriate laboratory controls. …[88]

"British healer Matthew Manning was able to exert dramatic negative influences on cervical cancer cells growing in culture, using appropriate laboratory controls. The negative influences occurred not only when he held a flask containing the cancer cells in his hands, but also when he tried mentally to influence them at a distance.[89]

"Jean Barry, a physician-researcher in Bordeaux, France, in a controlled study, demonstrated that people could inhibit the growth of a destructive fungus, *Rhizoctonia solani,* at a distance of 1.5 meters, using only mental intentions.[90]

"Barry's study was replicated by University of Tennessee researchers William H. Tedder and Melissa L. Monty, using the same organism, at a distance of one to fifteen miles, using student volunteers as influencers."[91]

Commenting on these studies Dossey observes, "The fact that these studies involve nonhumans is important, because this means that the results cannot be dismissed as due to suggestion or to the power of negative thinking."[92]

The cases of distant healing cited above seem to go against the laws of Newtonian physics and the wisdom of today's common sense. Are these, and many similar studies, a call for us to break down the centuries-old wall between science and religion?

GOD CANNOT BE MANIPULATED

The skeptics often have a very common traditional image of God as a being who is "out there" and is supposed to intervene or not intervene in the affairs of the world. Marcus Borg points out that quite often the Bible does speak of God as if God were a being "out there." He suggests that in the natural language of devotion, it is common to personify God because of the personal nature of the relationship. He points out that "the Bible also speaks of God as 'right here.'"[93] Borg quotes Psalm 139:

> You have searched me and known me;
> > you know when I sit down and when I rise up ...
> You go before me and behind me,
> > and lay your hand upon me ...
> Where can I go from your Spirit?
> > Or where can I flee from your presence?
> If I ascend to heaven, you are there;
> > if I make my bed in Sheol, you are there.
> If I take the wings of the morning and settle
> > at the farthest limits of the sea,
> > even there your hand shall lead me,
> > and your right hand shall hold me fast.

The affirmation is striking: no matter where one goes, God is there. How can that be? The answer comes, because everything is in God. There is no place one can be outside of God's presence. The skeptics assume a traditional, dualistic, "out there" or "up there" (while I'm down here) image of God taken from just one part of the Bible. They do not understand that God's grace cannot be located geographically because it is everywhere, mysterious and ineffable. We need to use nondualistic images of God drawn from other parts of the biblical tradition that are both metaphorical and paradoxical. In one of his letters from a Nazi prison, Dietrich Bonhoeffer put it this way: "God is the beyond in our midst."[94] This is not a logical statement but a paradox, a metaphor that tells us a good deal about the nature of God.

The skeptics are unacquainted with metaphorical, panentheistic images of God that claim that there is no place in the universe where God is not present. In these images of God there is no "out there," no manipulation, no arbitrary intervention. In Psalm 139, there is an enormous mystery about how God knows and cares about our human condition. However, this is not an image of a God who is apart from us.

If the skeptics could entertain a different, nondualistic, biblical image that suggests that everything is in God, that there is no place in the universe where God is not present, then they might have less difficulty examining the claims of distant healing. Paradox is necessary to illumine the panenthristic reality of God. Borg spells it out: "God is more than everything (and thus transcendent), yet everything is in God (hence God is immanent). For panentheism, God is 'right here,' even as God is more than right here."[95]

Galileo experienced the wrath of the Inquisition when he used his telescope and mathematical formulae to scientifically support the claim made by Copernicus that the Earth is not the center of the universe but travels around the sun. Galileo challenged foundational assumptions of his day and paid dearly for it.

Scientific support of healing at a distance has the potential of triggering a Copernican revolution of human consciousness in our time. Those who have observed and experienced the reality of distant healing need to understand what drives the skeptic. The truth of healing, if allowed into awareness, may threaten and shake the very ground upon which the skeptic stands.

HUMAN BROKENNESS AND GOD'S GRACE

Can God's grace touch our human brokenness in ways that technological medicine cannot? Here are two stories about this astonishing grace.

The first story began in the fall of 1989. Five months after I became the pastor of the Fairfax Community Church, United Church of Christ, in Fairfax, California, a retired nurse in the congregation received a diagnosis of cancer in the abdominal cavity. Her surgeon told her she had two months to live. She knew her condition was serious, but she also knew from her years of nursing experience that doctors can sometimes be wrong. She refused to lie down and die on schedule. She was a fighter: gutsy, hilariously funny, sometimes irreverent, and very courageous.

Eighteen months later she decided to accompany her husband on an archeological dig in Greece. Upon her return, we, several members of the congregation, formed a healing prayer group that met weekly in her home to pray with her for half an hour. She followed her oncologist's advice with a regime of chemotherapy. A year went by, two years, and then three as she held her own.

In the fourth year the cancer symptoms returned. During those last months of her life, I learned much about how one can face life's tragedies with courage and without complaint. Her "chutzpah" and humor never left her. She modeled an enormous strength of purpose for everyone around her. Without saying a word, she taught her friends and family how to die in style. We will be eternally in her debt. Her body was deteriorating, but her personhood was whole. She was not *cured*, but she most certainly died *healed*.

The second story is about a hospital chaplain intern who attended one of my retreats at a Roman Catholic center in July 1998. She had been living in significant pain for a number of years with lupus and rheumatoid arthritis. Most of her life revolved around one issue: how to minimize the pain and keep it at bay so that it did not dominate her whole life. She took 70 mg of prednisone every day, a very high dose. Everyone in the training receives a ten-minute healing from the group. When her turn came, she received about seven minutes of silent prayer. The ten of us then concluded with laying on of hands for about three minutes. During those ten minutes she received, by God's grace, a significant release from pain. It simply vanished. She was astonished, and group members were dumbfounded. There was a slight residue of pain, but three weeks later it was gone completely. It has not returned since July 1998.

A significant shift has occurred in her life. Several weeks later she told me that the most difficult part for her was how to find a new identity as a person whose life no longer revolved around fighting pain. Later, her general practitioner and rheumatologist were astonished and very curious. She told them about the prayers of the group and the laying on of hands. She stopped all medication, and the lab reports confirmed her cure. She has checkups every six months, and each time her physicians shake their heads in wonder.

It has been difficult for them to process this kind of experience because our culture's belief system does not equip us to understand the reality of sacred healing.

In my thirty years of teaching intercessory prayer, this kind of healing is very rare. All of the participants in the group were shaken by God's grace in action. People often receive benefit from the healing, but sometimes they don't experience anything. This story is told here because I want there to be an openness in the modern mind that says, "Yes, this kind of healing is possible." It is with some reluctance that I include this story of a dramatic healing because the validity of a healing does not need a dramatic result to be authentic.

In the dozen congregations on the West Coast where I have trained healing teams, a number of people come to healing stations, healing groups, or healing services each week. In reaching out for healing they open themselves to God and to Christ's presence. They feel loved, supported, and cared for because the Spirit is present, and they have taken the risk of opening themselves to God. They are not passive but proactive in their approach to healing. Month after month they feel rewarded and nurtured by a congregation that is a compassionate community. They do not need to have a remarkable healing. This book does not contain a large collection of stories about dramatic healings, though a few such accounts are included. Very rarely a dramatic healing does surprise us. Such a healing is deeply appreciated with a sense of gratitude, but it is not a test of the validity of the healing ministry. It is frosting on the cake.

The test of validity of a healing ministry in any congregation does not rest on whether or not cures have taken place. Sometimes a cure takes place as a result of healing prayer and sometimes not. Healing is a process that contains many elements. It is not defined alone by the presence or absence of a cure. For example, healing includes the loving support an ill person feels when receiving healing prayer or laying on of hands. The person often has a heightened ability to cope with the trauma and difficulty that accompany illness. Healing is often drawn out over days or weeks, rather than an instantaneous event. For those who care about the ill person, the offering of healing prayer erodes a sense of helplessness brought on by the belief that "nothing can be done." The person receiving healing prayer knows, in the midst of the isolation that pain brings, that she or he is not alone. That companionship supports and helps the ill person to endure and cope more effectively with the heavy, isolating reality of illness. All of these elements support the validity of healing prayer and cause us to make a necessary distinction between healing and curing.

HEALING AND CURING

How is the word *healing* used here? What does it mean? Here it is necessary to make a distinction between healing and curing. The word *heal* draws its meaning from the ancient Indo-European root word *kailo*, which means "whole, uninjured, of good omen."[96] The modern English words *hale, whole, wholesome, heal, holy, hallow, hello, healthy,* and *hail* can all be traced to that single root, *kailo,* whereas *cure* means "recovery from a disease."

Healing, as defined here, is the process of moving toward wholeness and does not depend on eliminating the disease. *Curing* is the eradication of disease. An individual may not be cured or curable and can still be in the process of healing. That person can still move toward wholeness, meaning, and well-being, like the retired nurse mentioned above. However, curing is not the polar opposite of healing, because sometimes curing happens in the midst of the healing process. The contrast between healing and curing is not an either/or category, but rather sometimes is a both/and situation.

Paradoxically an illness can even be a catalyst for healing, wholeness, and change. It can motivate one to pay attention to the dynamics of the mind and the soul. A friend of my wife, Virginia, received a diagnosis of cancer. After a year of treatment and reflection she said, "This cancer has been the best thing that has happened to me in years." After many years of estrangement from an adult daughter, they had become reconciled because of her life-threatening illness. She found new meaning in her life that she did not have before the cancer. She experienced wholeness and began to heal from the wounds of estrangement from her daughter. She was not cured, but she died healed.

Sometimes an illness is cured through prayer and sometimes not. There are really no good answers to the questions, "Why do some people benefit from healing prayer in body, mind, and soul and others not? Why do some benefit in mind and soul and not in the body?" Those questions have no answer. A few authors claim to know exactly why prayer was not effective and offer a psychological reason why the person was not cured. I find these claims overreaching and loaded with omniscience. It is necessary to live without answers—to live within the mystery of God's care—as did the author of Psalm 139, who asked many questions that had no answers.

HOW ONE VIEWS HEALING IS SPECIFIC TO THE CULTURE

In a larger context, healing is much more than alleviating a painful symptom. According to the Navajo, healing is a lifelong process that is holistic and cosmic. Nancy L. Maryboy and David H. Begay are Navajos who have studied traditional ways of healing expressed through Navajo consciousness. They are both faculty members in the Department of Physics and Astronomy at Northern Arizona University in Flagstaff. They observe that according to traditional Navajo understanding, healing is never complete.[97]

One never reaches a static plateau of perfection, a completely healthy state. Healing is a process, often a lifelong process. A healing is differentiated from a symptomatic cure, can be temporary or more permanent. It can be a temporary alleviation of pain or of a cluster of pain symptoms, or it can be a more permanent elimination of symptoms. However, a weak spot or mark may remain, and the illness can remanifest in another guise, sometimes years later.

I believe the Navajo view that healing is a restoration of balance that is an ongoing, lifetime process that is both holistic and cosmic. Certain spiritual practices in all cultures of the world give one access to the transcendent Holy. These practices used for healing vary widely, but each tradition can strengthen its own practice by selectively borrowing insights and spiritual practices from other traditions to illumine its own. My practice as a healer in the Christian tradition using intercessory prayer is deepened by the Navajo insight that healing is a lifetime process. This insight takes nothing away from my own understanding as a Christian that healing is a sign that the Kingdom of God is present in that moment. The Christian way of healing is effective and powerful, but it is not the only way.

Dr. Ulanov's words on intercessory prayer quoted at the beginning of the chapter describe my own experience and faith. "We enter a community held in God, framed by God, as well as finding God present to each of us directly in unmediated presence."

The practice of intercessory prayer creates a sacred space and allows the Spirit a deeper entrée into the lives of people and into the life of the larger congregation. There the Spirit can act with compassion in response to the pain and brokenness that are part of the web of life.

CHAPTER 9

Rediscovering Healing in the Twenty-First Century

> *Contemplative awareness reveals the wholeness that is present at the heart of reality. In our larger identity in God, we realize that coinherence; we taste its reconciling energy. It is out of that awareness in God raised to its fullness that Jesus radiated God's healing power. Again and again he called on people's faith in God's reconciling presence at every level of our being. The mind of faith is the mind that willingly opens to that personal presence.*[98]

> —Tilden Edwards

Healing, as Jesus practiced it and taught it to his followers, is evidence of the Good News that God loved the universe into being. God continues to express that love in our time through people who gather in prayer or contemplation to become open to the Holy. In so doing they create a spiritual community, or what can be sensed as a field of spiritual presence.

Jesus taught his followers to love: to love one another, to love the enemy, to love the disinherited, to love the self, and to love God with a full and focused intention. The question that has presented itself to Jesus's followers in every century is "Well, yes, I can support those teachings about love with my whole heart, but *how* does one go about doing it? *How* do you love?"

The practice of prayer for healing presents a concrete opportunity to learn *how* to practice compassion in the daily-ness of life. Praying with another person in pain is a concrete way to practice love. In previous chapters, a number of stories describe such compassion in the context of contemplative prayer. In chapter 3, John Dominic Crossan suggests that the disciples were probably among the first people Jesus healed. Crossan observes that they were "healed healers," and that their continuing practice of healing was their empowerment to heal others. They became a network of shared healing with Jesus.

EVERY APOSTLE A HEALER

Though healing was part of the core of Jesus's mission and message, he did not set aside certain disciples to offer healing as a specialty. He expected all of them to heal. Jesus was aware that God's gift of healing can be taught and developed. He sent out the apostles to do what he did: proclaim the good news of God's sovereignty and heal. The story of the epileptic boy whom Jesus healed when the disciples could not cure him suggests that Jesus offered them ongoing instruction in healing. An inference can be drawn here that he taught them how to heal and tutored them in their healing practice. How else would they have learned to offer healing? After Jesus healed the boy, the disciples asked him in the privacy of a nearby house, "Why could we not cast it out?" He said to them, "This kind can come out only through prayer" (Mark 9:14–29). Mark tells this story to show how Jesus instructed the disciples and how the center of gravity was extended from the healing power and deeds of Jesus to the participation of the disciples in that healing power. It can also be inferred that healing training originated when Jesus began to instruct the disciples in preparation for sending them out into the countryside to conduct the mission that he gave them.

CONFIDENCE IS NECESSARY AND DIFFICULT TO ACHIEVE

The confidence that one can become an instrument in God's hands for healing is difficult to come by in the mainline church today. That confidence did not come easily to Agnes Sanford, who has been called the "grandmother of the healing movement" in the United States. She considered herself a wounded healer. Her healing ministry began with the healing of her own depression of several years' duration. Later in her life, Morton Kelsey was her rector and worked with her in healing ministries for fifteen years. He describes the several elements that she considered essential for a healing ministry.[99] It began for her during the time she was depressed. She found someone who believed that spiritual healing was possible; she asked a Christian minister to lay hands on her for healing. Agnes recovered from her depression.

Where does one start? She believed that first it is necessary to find someone with "experience and background in the healing ministry to introduce us to its reality."[100] Her confidence to offer healing to others came out of her own experience of being healed. For any person in the church new to the subject, healing becomes possible when one seeks out an experienced healer. After her own healing, Agnes Sanford began praying with others in need at Trinity Episcopal Church in Moorestown, New Jersey, where her husband was the rector. She found that when she prayed and laid hands on people, many of them recovered. Sanford discovered she had a very powerful natural gift of healing. Very gifted healers often want to encourage and teach others to discover their own latent healing ability, which all people possess. She taught people how to offer healing prayer and called her training program the School of Pastoral Care, which she led in parishes around the country. In 1947, she wrote a book, *The Healing Light*, which I read when I was a junior in college.

EVERY PERSON IS A HEALER

You and I may not have a strong, natural gift of healing like Agnes Sanford, but one can develop the latent gift that every person has, to one degree or another. Every person is a healer, but that latent ability is not recognized. It has been my experience over the past thirty years that every person can develop the ability to heal with instruction and practice. This does not mean that people who do not take healing training cannot offer effective healing to others. They most certainly can.

Agnes Sanford and Ambrose and Olga Worrall were responsible for the healing of thousands of people through the use of their powerful gift over a fifty-year period. In addition, Olga founded the New Life Clinic at the Mt. Washington Methodist Church in Baltimore, which is still going strong today. She participated in dozens of scientific experiments that pointed to the evidence that spiritual healing does work. Ambrose was an aeronautical engineer for Martin Aircraft in Baltimore. I met Olga when we both served on the Executive Council of the Spiritual Frontiers Fellowship that met in Chicago during the early 1970s. In the Worrals' book, *The Gift of Healing*, Ambrose writes about the potential everyone has to be a healer:

> *Charisma* derives from a Greek word meaning "gift." The charismatic healer … is one who has a special gift, a power that he or she can use to heal others.
>
> Can only those who are gifted heal? This is like asking, Can a person who is not particularly gifted as an artist learn to paint? The answer is: Of course he can. Not perhaps in the measure of those described as masters of art, but often to a far greater degree than the individual himself may have thought possible. The same thing is true in the field of spiritual healing. The degree of *charisma* might be slight or great, it may be latent, it may be developed

or undeveloped, trained or untrained, primitive or sophisticated.[101]

Edgar N. Jackson, an authority on bereavement and author of *The Many Faces of Grief,* once told me how he was healed by Olga Worrall from a painful back injury he received while a chaplain in World War II. He was aboard an Army Air Corps hospital plane carrying wounded soldiers that crashed while landing. His back was broken, and he spent months in the hospital and was told by a number of specialists, over a period of months, that he would have to learn to live with the pain. There was nothing medical science could offer except pain medication. Upon discharge, he was disabled but able to serve a small Methodist Church in Corinth, Vermont. One Sunday, after the morning service, he was standing at the rear door of the sanctuary greeting parishioners as they left. Without any warning a woman asked him very pointedly, "Do you think that it is God's will that you continue to suffer this terrible back pain for the rest of your life?" He was astonished and mumbled something to the effect that no, he didn't think that was God's will. She then asked his permission to act as proxy for him when she attended a healing service the following Thursday morning, led by Olga Worrall at the New Life Clinic in Baltimore. He said he would appreciate that very much. Edgar woke up several days after the healing to discover that his back pain had vanished. In the many years after that healing, he did not experience a twinge of pain. Edgar went on to become a fine healer and wrote a book on the subject.

Not everyone can be Agnes Sanford or Olga or Ambrose Worrall, but each person has the ability to be an effective enabler of God's healing gift. However, those who have taken some form of healing training and who practice on a regular basis can become more powerful instruments in the hands of God. It seems to me that God loves to work with a tuned instrument. Individuals can become such an instrument by developing a willingness to pray and by giving themselves to God. It is necessary to get oneself out of the way so that the Holy can effect a transformation. It has been my experience that training in contemplative prayer exercises and a regular practice of offering healing prayer can deepen this process.

LACK OF CONFIDENCE

One of the greatest barriers to entering a ministry of healing, lay or clergy, is the feeling that "I do not have what it takes; my heart is not pure enough. I don't know enough or how to go about it." In today's skeptical world, it takes a certain amount of courage to follow Jesus the healer and imagine what he knew to be a fact: that every person has the latent ability to bring a degree of God's transformative healing to someone who is in pain. This is a continuation of Jesus's healing ministry that is practiced in our day, as the disciples practiced it in Jesus's day. When he sent them out two by two into the countryside, his presence was still with them when they began to heal. In the same way today, his presence can be with us when a person asks for him in a prayer of healing. The only thing necessary is to ask.

I remember the first time I offered prayer for healing with laying on of hands in the early 1970s. I had led healing prayer in small groups for a couple of years but never in a large healing service that included laying on of hands. I learned to do this at a national conference of Spiritual Frontiers Fellowship, which I had recently joined. Healing prayer was an accepted practice in that organization. During the conference, a friend led a large healing service that had about six healing stations. He asked me if I would like to serve at one of the stations, to offer prayer and to lay on hands. Inside I felt very uneasy. "Who, me? I'm just a beginner." I told him I didn't have much experience, though I did not tell him I had never laid on hands as part of a healing service. My friend said something to the effect of "That's okay; all you have to do is show up and pray. God does the healing part."

I have never forgotten my friend's encouragement and wisdom. What became clear in later years when I began to teach healing was that in the beginning, I did not need to have a lot of experience. All I needed to do was show up, ask for Christ's presence, offer a prayer to God from as deep a place as I could manage and remember that healing was possible. It was necessary to remember that the healing was from God, not from me. Here is a letter from a former student:

I am writing to connect with you after about 25 years. In July 1977 … I took a workshop on meditation and healing … During the workshop itself I experienced a healing of a chronic, repeating infection. And then, at the beginning of September, I landed in the hospital after being hit by a streetcar. I had broken ribs and a torn lung. At day 3, follow-up x-rays showed no break and no tear. My fellow workshop participants had been meeting and meditating for me. I tried for over a year to get my x-rays. After more than a year the hospital sent my Vermont doctor the second set, but said they had lost the first.

Now, I have a friend here in Vermont, who has been diagnosed with inoperable lung cancer. I am wondering if you have any students or former students in healing groups. I would like to be able to put her in touch with them. …

I think so fondly of my experience with you and the others. I look at that workshop as the beginning of my emotional healing … You played Pachelbel's Canon in D after a guided meditation. I had such an opening with that music. It felt like my heart was torn and I was flooded with feelings I had protected against all my life. I still remember seeing a double helix pulsing with colors moving up and down it. I wept and wept. Then, when we came back to process the experience, I said, "But it's only feelings." And you said, "Someone must have really done a number on you."

That was the beginning for me, Francis. Once my heart had broken open, I was on my way … In 1986, I returned to school and became a psychotherapist and have been practicing for 15 years. I do body/mind therapy and guide my clients in allowing their hearts to open to all the feeling they have protected themselves from.

Since that time with you, I have received other healings, most, though not all, emotional. I would like to help my friend find her way into the same kind of healing …

I hope you are well and that you have lived in the grace of all the healing you have introduced others to. You are among those whom I see as having taken me from one direction and moved me into another one …

Peace, Diane

Now and then students will be close to a turning point in their lives when they are drawn to the training. The intense contemplative prayer and meditation practice over five days opens them to a deeper level of awareness and allows the Holy to bring about significant transformations in their lives. As I reflect on Diane's gracious letter, it is clear to me that the Holy took her from one direction and moved her into another one. By God's grace she had discovered a deeper level of her God-self, her soul, because of her own contemplative practice and the prayers of the group. She generously credits me and the group with the transformation. However, we were not the source; the training that I led was a catalytic agent that enabled the Holy to transform and move her in another direction. In the words of my friend, "All you have to do is show up and pray. God does the healing part."

Like the woman who touched Jesus's cloak in the crowd, Diane opened herself to this possibility of transformation. At a very deep level, she wanted to be healed of the inner pain that burdened her life. This kind of transformation does not happen to very many students, but it does happen to some who seem to be at a turning point in their lives.

HEALING RESEARCH, 1974–76

Using this model of healing training, I conducted a study with four congregations in the mid-1970s under a foundation grant. It was the raw material for my dissertation project, "Healing Training in the Church," for the Doctor of Ministry degree at San Francisco Theological Seminary in San Anselmo, California. Eight to ten participants in each congregation agreed to attend the five-day training and then meet in a healing prayer group once a week for the next six months. During that period they also agreed to pray and meditate twenty minutes a day using these spiritual exercises. That was quite a commitment for some who had never practiced any form of meditation or contemplative prayer. During that six-month period there were a few dramatic healings in those four prayer groups. That did not surprise me, but what did catch my attention when interviewing participants six months later was the personal transformation a number of people reported as they followed a daily discipline of contemplative prayer and participation in a weekly healing prayer group.

One of the pastors in the study said, "When the group did the original healing with me at the training, … I remember the impact of experiencing unconditional love from God. That is still with me to the place where that assisted me in getting off a God who is out there counting my mistakes and is going to zap me in the end."[102]

Another subject in the study was concerned about her healing group's overemphasis on results. She said, "We all wanted some confirmation that what we were doing had some validity … a response from the ill person that they were getting better. In the back of my mind I was always expecting … some [recognizable] results. I [later] realized that if I believed in God … accepting God on faith … healing was just one of the things I was just going to have to accept on faith … that God was working in people's lives and that I needed nothing from this experience other than the doing of it. … Once I let go of the need for results … [and] expectations … then I sensed being closer to [those with whom I was praying.]"[103]

This person came to a profound understanding of ego involvement that can get in the way of healing: being preoccupied with results. She focused on the essential issue: God does the healing, not the healer.

Another person said, "I have gotten back into the spiritual side of my own faith and believing in a power that was greater than myself and being able to say [to God], 'You know I can't handle this right at this moment ... you do it ... and [I need to be] able to let go.' [The healing work] is being able to let it go and not get in there and try to fix it."[104] This person grasped the essence of healing prayer and described one of the main barriers to its effectiveness.

A number of subjects reported that their relationships to others had changed significantly over the six-month period. This was expressed as increased sensitivity, greater acceptance of others, and being less judgmental toward others. One man said to me, "I've noticed a greater sensitivity to people's feelings ... At times I feel like I'm really in touch with deeper levels of the person. ... My wife has commented on that. She says things like, 'I notice you don't get upset about little things as easily. You deal with them much more evenly.' I think that she has been conscious of greater affection that I've shown toward her. She said, 'It seems like we talk to one another more easily than we did ... that we share more things. ...This is a really big kind of personal benefit.'" This is a beautiful example of unexpected spiritual formation where it counts.

In drawing up the design for the healing training study, I anticipated that there would be some cases showing an accelerated rate of healing but was surprised to discover the variety and depth of spiritual formation and growth in participants during the six-month follow-up period.

THE VARIETIES OF HEALING PRAYER

Healing in the church today takes many different forms and is practiced in a variety of models. The model described here is similar to the others in that it is a continuation of the practice of healing that Jesus introduced two thousand years ago. It is difficult for the modern mind to wrap itself around the idea of spirit-energized healing. Healing should not be thought of as an irrational eruption of divine power into the orderly realm of nature. We know little about nature compared with what we do not know.

In the *City of God*, St. Augustine says that we have limited knowledge about many things. He offers a rather "scientific" explanation for understanding the meaning of a miracle, which he calls *portent*, which at first glance seems contrary to nature. "For we say that all portents [miracles] are contrary to nature; but they are not so. For how is that contrary to nature which happens by the will of God, since the will of so mighty a Creator is certainly the nature of each created thing? A portent therefore happens not contrary to nature, but contrary to what we know [about] nature."[105] The astronaut Edgar Mitchell puts the same idea in modern language: "There are not unnatural or supernatural phenomena, only very large gaps in our knowledge of what is natural."[106]

Healing in our time, healing training in the church, and the healing described in the biblical record is in no way contrary to nature, but contrary to what we know about nature. Today there is considerable ignorance about the laws of spirit-energized healing. These laws are in no way contrary to the natural order as known today scientifically, but they are still hidden, beyond our limited understanding of nature and beyond our present limited awareness of spiritual laws.

WHERE DOES ONE GO FROM HERE?

How does one begin to pray for others who are in pain? Offering prayer for healing and for the release from pain is probably not a new experience for the reader. The question is, How can one go deeper and become more effective as an instrument of God's healing gift and Christ's healing love?

A way to begin is to visit congregations in your community that offer a ministry of healing. That ministry may be practiced in several forms: a special weekly or monthly healing service where burdened individuals or those in pain can come for prayer and laying on of hands, a healing prayer circle, or receiving prayer and laying on of hands during the Sunday morning service. After any of these services or group meetings, ask one of the leaders how this kind of healing ministry began. Describe your interest and find the person or people in the congregation who have the most experience with and knowledge about healing. Sometimes it will be the pastor, other times an experienced layperson. Ask about other congregations in the community that offer a ministry of healing.

Discuss your interest in healing with your own pastor or laypeople who might have an interest in or experience with healing. If you are a pastor, seek out a fellow pastor in the community with experience in healing. Read several books on the literature of healing found in the bibliography. For example, *Stretch Out Your Hand* by Tilda Norberg and Robert Webber is an excellent introductory guide that was written as a study book for congregations. Norberg is a psychotherapist in New York with a seminary background, and Webber is a New Testament professor at Lancaster Theological Seminary in Pennsylvania. Using this book in a study group is an excellent way to introduce healing into the life of a congregation.

It has been my experience that the most effective healing happens in groups of people praying together. Similar to congregations in New Testament times, healing needs to be practiced as an expression of the entire faith community. One-on-one individual healing is certainly effective, but healing practiced in a group or in a healing service uses the significant power of the community focused in prayer.

I suggest that you ask permission to pray with or for someone who is in pain or under stress. These prayers can be offered in the person's presence or at a distance. When you ask permission, the person in pain knows that you are offering prayers for their recovery. They are touched by the offer as an expression of love. As Agnes Sanford has said, "It is love that fuels the healing fire." This expression of love is the first part of the healing.

HEALING IN THE TWENTY-FIRST CENTURY

In the twenty-first century, both scientists and healers are searching ever more intently to understand the natural laws of spirit-energized healing as they explore the vast mystery of the relationship between health and human consciousness. It has been my experience that healing prayer offered by a group, or an individual, can accelerate the self-repair mechanisms of a person who is ill or in pain. Every individual has a personal "healing system" that functions twenty-four hours a day to keep the human systems balanced and in good health. However, the human condition is often affected by pain and suffering. As noted earlier, Eugene O'Neill observed in *The Great God Brown* that "We are born broken. We live by mending. The grace of God is glue!" Healing training enables the person praying, by God's grace, to respond to the pain and suffering in the world as a continuation of a healing ministry that Jesus introduced long ago. The enabler/healer is also mended, healed, and becomes more whole in the process of offering healing prayer to another as a regular spiritual practice.

JESUS'S HEALING MINISTRY CONTINUES INTO OUR DAY

The healing training of the apostles began when Jesus instructed and tutored them to heal as an expression of the unlimited love that radiates from the Kingdom of God. It seems to me that in addition to Jesus's encouragement and continuing presence, it was their practice of healing that provided them confidence that God could use them in the healing of others.

How can we become, to use Crossan's words, "a network of shared healing with Jesus"? Being part of such a network begins with love. As stated at the beginning of chapter 8, "Love is the root energy hidden in all creation. In our brokenness we are recreated, healed, made whole by love's presence." To pray is to access that root energy of love by focusing our *intention* toward the source of that love, God. To pray with an ill person is to focus our *intention* toward the Holy,

136

asking that this person be included in our loving connection to God. In our tradition, we believe that God is the source of wholeness—the source of healing—the source of unlimited love that has no conditions. Where and how did we learn this: that *wholeness, healing*, and *love without conditions* can transform illness into wellness?

We learned that directly from Jesus, who was an exemplar of God's loving sovereignty and compassionate rule that he called the Kingdom of God. The teaching story of the prodigal son might well be called the story of the compassionate father, because it is a story about the father's unlimited, unconditional love for his youngest son who took his inheritance out into the world and messed up his life. We learn that love is the reuniting energy, not only from the teaching stories that Jesus told, but also in the way he demonstrated that God's unlimited love is not abstract but concrete. He embodied and modeled that unlimited love in relationships to those around him. The energy of that love continues to radiate into the wounded world today. This is continuing evidence of the Good News that God loved the world into being.

Pastor Jim Moiso, whom I interviewed in chapter 4, read the manuscript of this book before publication. Just before a healing service, he asked the healing prayer team to reflect on these words by Larry Dossey, MD, in the afterword: "We should remember that the greatest contribution of prayer to human welfare is *not* the eradication of disease but the restoration of wholeness, and the most majestic function of prayer is its capacity to be a bridge to the Absolute." In his letter to me, Moiso observed, "It helped us to remember who we are and what we are about."

Time and again those deeply burdened individuals who have received healing in the group have expressed profound gratitude for the love and support they have experienced after their healing. They have been touched deeply. You can see it in their eyes and hear it in their voices as they thank me and the group. My response is to thank them for the opportunity to pray with them and to remind them that what they are feeling so deeply is the support and love coming from the Spirit at work in our midst. As those offering healing prayer, we are only the conduits. God and Christ are the healers.

EPILOGUE

Healing a Wounded World

If all healing begins with pain, and if every person has some capacity to alleviate the pain of others, then every human being is a potential healer who can practice compassion. The holy force/energy that Jesus and his apostles mediated for the healing of a wounded person is the same holy energy that can help heal a sick society that is in pain. The healing just takes a different form. The Jesus-inspired healing energy that came through Martin Luther King Jr. addressed the painful sickness of racism in this country with a radical nonviolent love.

Healing the woundedness of institutions such as governments, churches, higher education, corporations, and others is sometimes influenced by the transformation of individual consciousness in small groups than can lead to a change in national or global consciousness. Inspired by Jesus, Dr. King was a healer who sought to bring justice and peace to the pain-wracked conflicts of racism and the Vietnam War. The Dalai Lama has observed, "Although attempting to bring about world peace through the internal transformation of individuals is difficult, it is the only way … Peace must first be developed within an individual. And I believe that love, compassion, and altruism are the fundamental basis for peace. Once these qualities are developed within an individual, he or she is then able to create an atmosphere of peace and harmony. This atmosphere can be expanded and extended from the individual to his family, from the family to the community and eventually to the whole world."[107]

Global healing starts with individual healing. The two forms of healing are clearly connected, part of a single whole if viewed through the lens of a "quantum reality." It is clear to me that the practice of healing prayer described in this book brings about the "internal transformation of individuals" described by the Dalai Lama. That transformation helps to bring healing to a wounded world. In the Christian tradition, Jesus introduced healing as a sign of the Good News of God, a transformational spiritual practice grounded in love. Love is the root energy that is hidden in all creation.

The congregation is a healing community that expresses the root energy of love in a concrete way. Through prayer for others, the church is enabled to function more effectively as the body of Christ in the world.

AFTERWORD

Larry Dossey, MD

I belong to a profession that once honored the role of prayer and spirituality in healing but that abandoned that perspective almost completely during the twentieth century. This occurred as a result of medicine's head-over-heels infatuation with empirical science and physical approaches to health, such as vaccines, antibiotics, and surgery. *Healing,* as Francis Geddes uses the term in this fine book, simply became irrelevant. Healing was simply something a wound or an abrasion did, not a process related to the wholeness of a human being. Gradually, healing became a purely physical process that proceeded automatically, following the so-called blind laws of nature in which consciousness, intention, and compassion were said to have no place. *Healer* also vanished from medicine. During my stint in medical school, if someone had called us students healers, we would not have known if we were being praised or damned.

As Geddes makes clear, however, this situation, fortunately, is changing. We are again embracing healing on many levels in our society, including health care. In 1993, for instance, only three of the nation's 125 medical schools had courses in which the role of spirituality in health care was discussed. Today, around a hundred medical schools have such. Though controversial in some quarters, this change is dramatic and reflects a return to medicine's historical roots.

There are many reasons for this transition. People increasingly view modern medicine as remote, cold, inhumane, unavailable, too expensive, and often too late. Everywhere there is a hunger for compassionate health care, for *caring*. Fueling this desire is widespread disenchantment with high-tech medicine and a pervasive sense that it has been oversold. For example, as a result of medical errors and the side effects of pharmaceutical drugs, hospital care has become the third leading cause of death in the United States, behind heart disease and cancer.[1] Although we should be grateful for the contributions of high-tech medicine, it is apparent that something has gone missing of late—something having to do with matters of the spirit.[2]

Geddes wisely calls attention to the emerging scientific evidence for healing. As he shows, an increasing number of controlled, double-blind experiments strongly suggest that the healing effect is real—even at a distance, when the recipient is unaware that the healing effort is being extended. Particularly remarkable are the scores of healing studies that have been conducted in animals, plants, bacteria, and fungi, and even on biochemical reactions in test tubes. These experiments bypass the most common criticism of prayer studies in humans, that the effects are caused only by suggestions, expectations, and positive thinking.[3]

A recent survey of healing research found more than 2,200 published reports, including books, articles, dissertations, abstracts, and other writings on spiritual healing, so-called energy medicine, and the effects of mental intention on nonhumans. This included 122 laboratory studies, 80 randomized controlled trials, 128 summaries or reviews, 95 reports of observational studies and nonrandomized trials, 271 descriptive studies, case reports, and surveys. Using strict criteria to measure the quality of this evidence, Dr. Wayne B. Jonas and researcher Cindy C. Crawford concluded that the evidence for remote healing studies, as well as studies involving inanimate devices, was "fair" and "good," respectively.[4]

This evidence remains little known. Unfortunately, some skeptics tend to single out an individual prayer experiment or two, condemn them to high heaven, and generalize to dismiss the entire field. In any other area of science this would be considered inappropriate and prejudicial, and it reveals the intellectual indigestion that the idea of distant healing continues to evoke in some quarters.

Why the opposition to prayer in healing? Philosopher Karen Armstrong describes in her landmark book *The Battle for God* how human beings have evolved two main ways of knowing, *mythos* and *logos*. Both methods were essential, and neither was complete without the other. *Mythos* was considered timeless and unchanging, and was the foundation for religion and spirituality. Its special area of competence was not practicality but *meaning*. It shed light on human origins, the purpose of life, the origins of culture, and human destiny after death. Its contribution to human welfare was absolutely essential. Modern research confirms that without an adequate source of meaning, humans fall into despair and often sicken and die. *Mythos* was a sustaining corrective to this tendency; it lent a depth and richness to life by directing one's inner gaze to the eternal and the universal.

In contrast, *logos* was concerned not with meaning but with practicality. It prized reason, intellectuality, analysis, and the human talent for problem solving. It converted the literal lessons of *mythos* into metaphor, and sought to understand the workings of the world outside of a religious context. Beginning in the 1600s, *logos* evolved into what we now call science, whereas *mythos* continued to be anchored as always in religion, revelation, and mystical experience. After the European Enlightenment, *logos* became the dominant way of knowing for millions of Westerners, who were convinced that *mythos* had served its purpose and could be safely retired.

But although the ancient myths were dismissed, the human need for meaning did not disappear. Hungering for a new source of meaning, modern humans invented new myths to sustain them, as humans have always done. One of these is the belief that science is a sufficient explanation for all there is. This often involves *scientism*, which is the cloaking of one's personal views in the robes of science in an attempt to justify one's personal convictions about how the world *ought* to work. Those who adhere to scientism know in advance how the universe should behave, and they are impatient with anyone who produces evidence that says otherwise. This gambit, of course, is not science, which is value-neutral and was never intended to answer questions of meaning and purpose. But the dogmas of scientism have become all too common in many areas of science, and they sometimes reveal themselves in the objections of scientists to prayer and healing.

Is Geddes correct in emphasizing how "intercessory prayer meets science"? Some clergy don't think so, arguing that "it is a sin to test God."[6] Yet I know of no researchers in this field who are trying to test, prove, or disprove the Almighty in these studies. One researcher I know says that when she does her experiment, she is "opening a window to the Divine," who may enter—or not. Another researcher describes her laboratory as "holy ground." This reflects the view of most researchers in this field that they are dealing with sacred science.

Prayer research reflects the earliest traditions of science, described by philosopher Jacob Needleman in his book *A Sense of the Cosmos*.[7] When science first arose, he says, the first scientists wanted to bypass the word of the church about how nature worked. They wanted to prove for themselves how things behaved, with no in-between arbiter. Their goal was to have a personal, unmediated experience of the natural world and the Supreme Being who governed it. This urge, says Needleman, was decidedly spiritual and resembled the universal mystical urge—for a mystic is someone who also desires an unmediated experience of the Absolute.

In doing prayer experiments, modern researchers are following the path of the earliest scientists—bypassing religious authority and doctrine, seeing for themselves how prayer and healing work— and doing so respectfully. What have they found? In addition to Geddes's summary, I wish to emphasize three results that stand out. Researchers have discovered that individuals who are prayed for respond positively, statistically speaking, compared with those not assigned prayer, in a variety of diseases. It is to be emphasized that these results are statistical, meaning they are not invariable; statistical responses are the foundation of modern medical research. The researchers have also found that the religious affiliation of the praying person seems not to matter; nonaffiliated intercessors are as effective as religious ones. Furthermore, they have discovered that love and compassion seem to be the most important factors in the success of these experiments.

These findings pose great challenges for individuals who believe their religious tradition is uniquely favored where prayer is concerned. Thus far there is no evidence that any particular religion enjoys a monopoly on healing prayer. Prayer is universal, belonging to the entire human race, not to specific traditions.

We should celebrate this fact, for it is an endorsement of religious tolerance. This is one of the greatest contributions of the healing experiments, for in our post-9/11 world, religious tolerance is in short supply—not just in the Islamic world but also in our own country, where religious fundamentalism is enjoying a renaissance.

A few years ago I gave a lecture on healing research to the staff of a large hospital in New York City. Later that day I addressed the hospice workers in that same institution. A clergyman, who worked on the hospice unit full-time, offering spiritual counseling and prayer to patients and hospice staff alike, approached me with a troubled look. "I attended your talk on the research in prayer and healing this morning," he said. "I have to get one thing straight. Are you claiming that prayer actually *works*?" This man, whose entire life was characterized by prayer, had profound doubts about the effectiveness of his efforts. Prayer for him had become little more than a bland ritual that conveyed comfort but little more. His response is typical of the doubt shared by many these days. I am convinced that prayer science can be restorative, invigorating, and inspiring to these individuals. Even believers in prayer's healing potential can have their beliefs affirmed and strengthened by engaging this evidence.

Still, there are caveats. We should never hold prayer hostage to science, because science is limited in what it can lay hold of. The great wisdom traditions will always have a role to play—the *major* role—in spiritual matters, including prayer. Perhaps the greatest risk in prayer-and-healing is over-enthusiasm. We can become a cheerleader for any closely held belief, including the role of prayer in healing. When this happens, there is a tendency to take a purely concrete, utilitarian approach in which prayer becomes merely the latest tool in our black bag. We should remember that the greatest contribution of prayer to human welfare is *not* the eradication of disease but the restoration of wholeness, and that the most majestic function of prayer is its capacity to be a bridge to the Absolute.

Many congregations in our land would be utterly shocked to see prayer heal. Francis Geddes's book challenges these groups to engage the evidence for prayer's potential in healing, thereby reclaiming the promise of healing that is central to the legacy of Christianity. But Geddes's vision is ecumenical and universal—without which authentic healing and wholeness are an oxymoron.

Geddes shows that genuine healing can express itself in many ways—not only as the wholeness of an individual, but also of societies, nations, and the world. This expanded vision of healing is urgently needed. For, in matters of healing—whether of the enmities and hatreds that inflame passions and create wars, or of our fractured environment, or of the millions around the world from whose lives hope has departed—time is not on our side. That is why Geddes's book should not be read casually or at leisure, but given priority.

For the continued return of prayer, I pray.

—Larry Dossey, MD
Santa Fe, New Mexico

Notes to the Afterword

1. Starfield B. (2000). Is US health really the best in the world? *JAMA 284*(4), 483–485.

2. Dossey L. (2006). *The Extraordinary Healing Power of Ordinary Things*. New York: Bell Tower/Random House.

3. Dossey, L. (1993). *Healing Words: The Power of Prayer and the Practice of Medicine*. San Francisco: Harper San Francisco.

4. Jonas, W. B., & Crawford, C. C. (2003). *Healing, Intention and Energy Medicine*. New York: Churchill Livingstone: xv–xix.

5. Armstrong K. (2000*). The Battle for God*. New York: Ballantine: xv.

6. Dossey L., & Hufford D. (2005). Are prayer studies legitimate? Twenty criticisms. *Explore 1*(2): 109–117.

7. Needleman J. (1975). *A Sense of the Cosmos: The Encounter of Modern Science with Ancient Truth*. Garden City, NY: Doubleday: 167–170.

Notes

Scripture quotations, except where otherwise noted, are taken from *The New Revised Standard Version of the Bible,* Copyright 1989, by the Division of Christian Education of the National Council of the Churches of Christ in the United States of America.

Chapter 1, "On Being Drawn to Healing"

1. Larry Dossey, Foreword to *Miracles of Mind.* Russel Targ & Jane Katra, Novato, CA: New World Library, 1998, p. xi.

2. Raymond Arsenault, *Freedom Riders: 1961 and the Struggle for Racial Justice.* Oxford: Oxford University Press, 2006, p. 570.

Chapter 2, "Learning the Healing Practice"

3. Julian of Norwich, *Meditations with Julian of Norwich.* Brendan Doyle, trans. Santa Fe, NM: Bear & Co., 1983, p. 77.

4. Charles R. Ringma, *The Seeking Heart: A Journey with Henri Nouwen.* Brewster, MA: Paraclete, 2006, p. 78.

Chapter 3, "Jesus: The Healer Who Taught Healing"

5. Tilden Edwards, *Living in the Presence: Disciplines for the Spiritual Heart.* San Francisco: Harper & Row, 1987, p. 85.

6. Dietrich Bonhoeffer, *Letters and Papers from Prison*, "Outline for a Book," p. 202, quoted in Larry L. Rasmussen, *Dietrich Bonhoeffer: Reality and Resistance,* Nashville: Abingdon, 1972, reprinted Louisville, KY: Westminster John Knox, 2005, p. 21. Retrieved November 12, 2009, from Google Books.com.

7. Mary Ann Tolbert. Earle Lecture Workshop. Berkeley, CA: Pacific School of Religion, 1995.

8. Marcus J. Borg, *The Heart of Christianity*. San Francisco: Harper San Francisco, 2003, pp. 89–90.

9. Ibid., 90.

10. Mircea Eliade. *Shamanism*. Princeton, NJ: Princeton University Press, 1972, p. 4.

11. Ibid.

12. Marcus J. Borg, *Conflict, Holiness, and Politics in the Teachings of Jesus*. Harrisburg, PA: Trinity, 1984, p. 261.

13. John Bright, *The Kingdom of God*. New York: Abingdon, 1953.

14. Robert Funk, Roy W. Hoover, & the Jesus Seminar, *The Five Gospels*. New York: Macmillan, 1993, p. 531.

15. Elizabeth Schussler Fiorenza, *In Memory of Her*. New York: Crossroad, 1983, pp. 120–123.

16. John Dominic Crossan, *Jesus: A Revolutionary Biography*. San Francisco: Harper San Francisco, 1994, p. 93.

17. Ibid., 109.

18. John Wilkinson, *The Bible and Healing: A Medical and Theological Commentary.* Grand Rapids. MI: Wm. B. Erdmans, 1998, p. 189.

19. Borg, *Conflict, Holiness*, op. cit., 261–262.

20. Ibid., 262.

21. Walter Wink, *Engaging the Powers.* Minneapolis: Fortress, 1992, pp. 5–6.

22. Wilkinson, *The Bible and Healing*, op. cit., 189.

23. Ibid., 237–238.

24. Ibid., 259.

25. Ibid., 260.

26. Ibid. 257.

27. Marcus J. Borg, *Jesus: Uncovering the Life, Teachings, and Relevance of a Religious Revolutionary.* San Francisco: Harper San Francisco, 2006, p. 25.

28. Ibid., 28.

29. John P. Meier, *A Marginal Jew: Rethinking the Historical Jesus*, vol. 2, *Mentor, Message, and Miracles.* New York: Doubleday, 1994, p. 630.

30. William R. Herzog, *Prophet and Teacher: An Introduction to the Historical Jesus.* Louisville, KY: Westminster John Knox, 2005, pp. 19–20.

31. Ibid., 25–26.

32. Ibid., 26.

33. Ibid., 26–27.

34. Ibid., 27.

35. Ibid.

36. Ibid.

37. Ibid.

38. Borg, Ibid., *Jesus: Uncovering the Life*, 25.

39. Wilkinson, op. cit., 88.

40. *The Book of Common Prayer, According to the Use of the Episcopal Church.* 1979, p. 456.

41. Eugene O'Neill. *The Great God Brown.* New York: Boni & Liveright, 1926, act 4, scene 1.

Chapter 4, "Integrating Healing into a Parish"

42. Gerald G. May, MD, *Addiction and Grace.* San Francisco: Harper & Row, 1988, p. 154.

43. John Dominic Crossan, "Jesus As a Mediterranean Jewish Peasant," *The Fourth R,* 1991. Sonoma, CA: Jesus Seminar, p. 12.

44. Crossan, *A Revolutionary*, op. cit., 109.

45. Ibid., 195–196.

46. William E. Swing, column in *Pacific Church News*. San Francisco: Diocese of California, 2002.

47. Dean Ornish, MD, "Opening Your Heart: Anatomically, Emotionally, and Spiritually," in *Consciousness and Healing: Integral Healing Approaches to Mind-Body Medicine*, Marilyn Schlitz et al., eds. St. Louis: Elsevier, 2005, p. 405.

Chapter 5, "Healing Transforms Clergy"

48. Martin Buber, *Hasidism and Modern Man*. New York: Horizon, 1958, pp. 112–113.

49. Lawrence LeShan, *How to Meditate*. Boston: Little, Brown, 1974.

50. Agnes Sanford, *The Healing Light*. St. Paul, MN: Macalester Park Publishing, 1949, p. 52.

Chapter 6, "Laity Experience Transformation in Healing"

51. Carl G. Jung, *Letters*, August 20, 1945, quoted in Larry Dossey, *Healing Words: The Power of Prayer and the Practice of Medicine*. New York: HarperPaperbacks, 1997 (first published in 1993), p. 111.

52. Crossan, *A Revolutionary,* op. cit., 109.

Chapter 7, "Prayer Meets Science: Cooperation, Not Conflict"

53. David Bohm, quoted in Russell Targ & Jane Katra, *Miracles of Mind*. Novato, CA: New World Library, 1998, p. 273.

54. *Spirituality & Healing in Medicine*. Announcement of a Two-Day Course, Harvard Medical School, December 2004.

55. Larry Dossey, MD, Afterword to *Contemplative Healing: The Congregation as Healing Community,* by Francis Geddes.

56. Larry Dossey, MD. *Reinventing Medicine: Beyond Mind-Body to a New Era of Healing.* San Francisco: Harper San Francisco, 1999, p. 43. [study citation: Bernard R. Grad, "Some Biological Effects of Laying-On of Hands: A Review of Experiments with Animals and Plants," *Journal of the American Society for Psychical Research, 59a,* 1965: 95–127.]

57. Ibid., 53. [study citation: Randolph C. Byrd, "Positive Therapeutic Effects of Intercessory Prayer in A Coronary Care Unit Population," *Southern Medical Journal, 81*(7), 1988: 826–829.]

58. Daniel J. Benor, MD, republished as *Spiritual Healing: Scientific Validation of a Healing Revolution, Healing Research Vol. 1 (Popular Edition & Professional Supplement).* Bellmawr, NJ: Wholistic Healing Publications, 2002. http://wholistichealingresearch.com.

59. Dossey, Foreword to *Miracles of Mind*, Targ & Katra, op. cit, p. xi.

60. Gary Zukav, *The Dancing Wu Li Masters.* New York: Wm. Morrow, 1979, pp. 42–43.

61. Mike Denney, Walking the Quantum Talk *IONS Noetic Sciences Review, 13* (June–August, 2002), p. 19.

62. Ibid., 19–20.

63. Larry Dossey, *Reinventing, op. cit.,* 19–20.

64. Ibid., 24.

65. Ibid.

66. Ibid.

67. J. Philip Newell, *Celtic Prayers from Iona*. New York/Mahwah, NJ: Paulist, 1997, p. 40.

68. Dossey, Ibid., 25.

69. Ibid., p. 25

70. Larry Dossey, MD, "Healing and the Nonlocal Mind," interview by Bonnie Horrigan, *Alternative Therapies in Health and Medicine*, 5(6), 1999, p. 87.

71. Lawrence LeShan, *The Medium, The Mystic, and the Physicist*. New York: Viking, 1974, p. 158.

72. Julian of Norwich, *Meditations*, op. cit., 93, 17.

73. Julian of Norwich, *Julian of Norwich Showings*. Edmund College, O.S.A. & James Walsh, S.J., eds. and trans. New York: Paulist, 1978, p. 128.

74. Dossey, *Reinventing*, op. cit., 25.

75. David Spiegel, "Effects of Psychosocial Treatment on Survival of Patients with Metastatic Breast Cancer," *The Lancet 2*, 1989: 888–891.

76. Thomas Lewis, Fari Amini, & Richard Lannon, *A General Theory of Love*. New York: Vintage, 2000, p. 220.

77. *Life*, New York (1996, June), 18.

78. Agnes Sanford, quoted by LeShan, *Medium*, op. cit., 107.

Chapter 8, "Healing Is the Practice of Compassion"

79. Ann Belford Ulanov in *A Review of Scientific and Pastoral Perspectives on Intercessory Prayer: An Exchange Between Larry Dossey, M.D. and Health Care Chaplains.* Larry Vande Creek, ed. Binghampton, NY: Haworth Press Prepublication review, 1998, facing the title page.

80. Tom Harpur, *The Uncommon Touch: An Investigation of Spiritual Healing.* Toronto: McClelland & Stewart, 1994, p. 20.

81. Patricia Swanson Megregian, *A Review of Scientific and Pastoral.* op. cit., 108–109.

82. Robert Funk, et al., *The Five Gospels*, op. cit., p. 145.

83. LeShan, *The Medium,* op. cit., 143.

84. Ibid., 158.

85. Teresa of Avila, *Interior Castle*, 6th Mansions, chapter 8, ¶ 4, quoted in Gerald C. May, MD, *The Dark Night of the Soul: A Psychiatrist Explores the Connection Between Darkness & Spiritual Growth.* New York: HarperCollins, 2004.

86. Julian of Norwich, *Meditations,* op. cit., 77.

87. Dossey, *Reinventing,* op. cit., 154.

88. Glen Rein, *Quantum Biology: Healing with Subtle Energy.* Palo Alto, CA: Quantum Biology Research Labs, 1992.

89. William Braud, Gary Davis, & Robert Wood, "Experiments with Matthew Manning," *Journal of the Society for Psychical Research 50*, 1979: 199–223.

90. Jean Barry, "General and Comparative Study of the Psychokinetic Effect on a Fungus Culture," *Journal of Parapsychology 32*(4), 1968: 237–243.

91. William H. Tedder & Melissa L. Monty, "Exploration of Long-Distance PK: A Conceptual Replication of the Influence on a Biological System," in *Research in Parapsychology 1980,* ed. W. G. Roll et al. Metuchen, NJ: Scarecrow, 1981, pp. 90–93.

92. Dossey, 154–155.

93. Marcus J. Borg, *The God We Never Knew: Beyond Dogmatic Religion to a More Authentic Contemporary Faith.* San Francisco: Harper San Francisco, 1997, pp. 34–36.

94. Ibid., 46–47.

95. Ibid., 32.

96. *The American Heritage Dictionary of the English Language,* William Morris, ed. Boston: Houghton Mifflin, 1971, p. 1520.

97. Nancy C. Maryboy & David H. Begay, "Restoration of Dynamic Balance: Traditional Ways of Healing Expressed Through Navajo Consciousness," in *Consciousness and Healing,* op. cit., 405.

Chapter 9, "Rediscovering Healing in the Twenty-First Century"

98. Tilden Edwards, *Living in the Presence, Disciplines for the Spiritual Heart.* San Francisco: Harper & Row, 1987, p. 85.

99. Morton Kelsey, *Psychology, Medicine, and Christian Healing* (also published as *Healing and Christianity*). San Francisco: Harper & Row, 1988, pp. 314–315.

100. Ibid., 314.

101. Ambrose A. Worrall & Olga N. Worrall, *The Gift of Healing*. Columbus, OH: Ariel, 1985, p. 192.

102. Francis Geddes, *Healing Training in the Church*. San Anselmo, CA: San Francisco Theological Seminary, unpublished dissertation, 1981, p. 122.

103. Ibid., 123.

104. Ibid., 126.

105. St. Augustine, *Basic Writings of St. Augustine*, Vol. 2. Whitney J. Oaks, ed. New York: Random House, 1948, p. 575.

106. Edgar Mitchell, quoted in Elizabeth Rauscher, "Science, Mysticism, and the New Tomorrow," *Bridges Quarterly Magazine 17*(1), Spring, 2006, p. 20, International Society for the Study of Subtle Energy & Energy Medicine.

107. The Dalai Lama quoted in Gerald G. May, MD, in "From Cruelty to Compassion" in *Deepening the American Dream: Reflections on the Inner Life and Spirit of Democracy*, Mark Nepo, ed. New York: Jossey-Bass/Wiley, 2005, p. 372.

Annotated Bibliography

Benor, Daniel J., MD, *Healing Research, Vol. 1, Spiritual Healing: Scientific Validation of a Healing Revolution (Popular Edition & Professional Supplement).* Bellmawr, NJ: Wholistic Healing Publications, 2002.

Psychiatrist, healer, and founder of the Doctor-Healer Network in England and North America, Dr. Benor has provided the most thorough scientific survey of healing now in print. It includes a variety of anecdotal reports or methods and positive results of healing: healers' views on healing; psi phenomena; 131 scientifically controlled experiments of healers' effects on the physical world; and laboratory studies of healing action on bacteria, plants, animals, and human beings. More than half of these studies showed statistically significant results, yet they are ignored or rejected by most mainstream scientist. One can only ask, "Why?" Benor suggests that "Many critics would cloud the evidence with any excuses to support their disbelief rather than examine either the phenomena or their own discomforts with them." This is a small encyclopedia of healing practice, research, and theory. It is very meaty and has become a classic study in the field. Dr. Benor is editor of the online *International Journal of Healing and Caring.* Online address: http://wholistichealingresearch.com.

Borg, Marcus J., *Jesus: A New Vision.* New York: Harper and Row, 1987.

———. *Meeting Jesus Again for the First Time: The Historical Jesus and the Heart of Contemporary Faith.* San Francisco: Harper San Francisco, 1994.

———. *The God We Never Knew: Beyond Dogmatic Religion to a More Authentic Contemporary Faith.* San Francisco: Harper San Francisco, 1997.

———. *The Heart of Christianity: Rediscovering a Life of Faith.* San Francisco: Harper San Francisco, 2003.

———. *Jesus: Uncovering the Life, Teachings, and Relevance of a Religious Revolutionary.* Harper San Francisco: 2006.

In these five books Borg presents the pre-Easter Jesus as a Jewish *mystic, healer, teacher of wisdom, social prophet,* and *movement founder.* "According to the gospels he had visions, fasted, spent long hours in prayer, spoke of God in intimate terms, and taught the immediacy of access to God—something mystics know in their own experience … The mighty deeds of Jesus, exorcisms and healings alike, were the product of the power that flowed through him as a holy man. His powers were charismatic, the result of his having become a channel for the power of the other realm, that which Jesus and his contemporaries also called Spirit." Borg observes that Jesus' healing was a manifestation of this sacred reality, the Spirit in action, which was clear evidence that the Kingdom of God was at hand. Healing prayer that invites the presence of the post-Easter Jesus is a resource for God's transformative power. Borg is one of the very few New Testament scholars who present Jesus as a visionary/healer who ventures into other dimensions of reality, which is "the classic experience of the shaman." *The God We Never Knew* provides an illuminating thread of continuity from the pre-Easter Jesus to the post-Easter Jesus, to the creeds of the fourth century, dominated by Greek thought. In *Jesus: Uncovering the Life, Teachings, and Relevance of a Religious Revolutionary, the book's dust jacket says,* "Marcus Borg takes us on an incredible journey to discover who Jesus was, what he taught, and why he still matters today. In the definitive book of his career, Borg argues that how we see Jesus affects how we see Christianity and reveals a new way of seeing—between the literalists and progressives, a path that emphasizes following 'the way' of Jesus, the original name of the Jesus movement."

Crossan, John Dominic, *Jesus, A Revolutionary Biography.* San Francisco: Harper San Francisco, 1994.

This volume is the distillation of Crossan's lifelong scholarship focused on the historical Jesus. In the United States he is the preeminent authority in this field. He sees Jesus' healing as a significant part of his total ministry, like no other New Testament scholar. This author's only disagreement is that he tends to psychologize Jesus' healings as a kind of placebo effect rather than real cures of real physical illness. Crossan seems not to be acquainted with the solid scientific research on healing prayer (such as Daniel Benor above or Larry Dossey below) that rules out the placebo effect as an explanation. Jesus brought about physical cures by the power of God coming through his hands and heart.

Dossey, Barbara Montgomery, R.N., M.S., *Florence Nightingale— Mystic, Visionary, Healer.* Springhouse, PA, Springhouse Corporation, 2000.

Dossey observes, "Like a fiery comet, Florence Nightingale streaked across the skies of 19th century England and transformed the world with her passage." Many people are not aware that she was a God-saturated woman. Her lifelong desire to serve God came to her after a spiritual awakening when she was sixteen. As a young woman she almost single-handedly fashioned nursing into a respected profession in the English-speaking parts of the world. She established the first school for training nurses in England. Not only was she responsible for providing heroic nursing care to wounded soldiers in the Crimean war hospitals, but she later saved thousands of lives in England because she was able to persuade influential members of Parliament and the Cabinet to bring modern sanitation reforms to the entire country, which drank polluted water and suffered from primitive sewage disposal systems. She was one of the founders of statistical analysis that she developed in analyzing patient recovery rates and death rates in British Army hospitals. She was a behind-the-scenes political activist on many fronts, using her brilliant mind, courage, and compassion. She worked with those who sought to bring about independence for India in the first decade of the twentieth century. Throughout her life, at the beginning of each day, she sought to discover what God wanted her to do. Because she modeled such a deep surrender to God's purpose for her life, this author is inspired and feels great affection and admiration for her selfless efforts to alleviate suffering and pain in whatever form it took. As you read this book, Florence Nightingale will come alive and become an inspiring companion on your spiritual journey.

Dossey, Larry, MD, *Healing Words: The Power of Prayer and the Practice of Medicine.* San Francisco: Harper San Francisco, 1993.

This book reveals one of the best-kept secrets in medical science: prayer heals. It helps to restore the spiritual art of healing to the science of medicine. This volume is the provocative, courageous, and powerfully instructive result of Dossey's quest to rethink his own spiritual life and discover what works best for his patients. Citing compelling studies and fascinating case histories, Dossey shows how prayer complements, but does not take the place of, good medicine. He describes how prayer manifests in laboratory experiments, and how modern physics contributes to understanding them. "Part Two: Factors Influencing the Efficacy of Prayer" is one of the best descriptions of intercessory prayer in print. He introduces us to the language of the new physics when he calls prayer at a distance "nonlocal" healing. This author is persuaded that Dossey is what Marcus Borg describes as a "spirit person." If you read only one book listed here, let it be this one.

Gaynor, Mitchell L., MD, *Sounds of Healing.* New York: Broadway Books, 1999.

Dr. Gaynor began to meditate when he was an undergraduate. He found medical school stressful, in part because the medical culture insisted that he keep an emotional distance from the patient. Today he is the director of oncology and integrative medicine at the Strang-Cornell Cancer Prevention Center in New York City. In 1991, he was asked by another attending physician to evaluate a new patient, a Tibetan monk, with a serious heart problem. After several visits, Dr. Gaynor asked Odsal to teach him some chants. At that time, Odsal brought a Tibetan singing bowl and moved a wood baton around its rim. Gaynor describes his reaction: "The clamor of the New York City streets, so audible outside my window, fell away as the eerie otherworldly tones of the bowl filled the space around us. The sound—a rich, deep note with a strong vibrato that resembled nothing that I had ever heard before—was so exhilarating that tears of joy sprang to my eyes. I could feel the vibration physically resonating through my body, touching my core in such a way that I felt in harmony with the universe." Throughout the book, he explains how sound, in different forms, can be a source of healing. He describes the implications of entrainment, harmony, and homeostasis as well as the power of music and voice. Throughout his story, the reader becomes aware that not only is he a compassionate physician and researcher, but his exploration into new areas of healing is also part and parcel of his spiritual path. He quotes Lawrence LeShan that there is a song inside of us that needs to be sung. Our job is to discover what it is and then sing.

Graham, Rochelle, Flora Litt, and Wayne Irwin, *Healing from the Heart: A Guide to Christian Healing for Individuals and Groups.* Winfield, B.C., Canada: Wood Lake Books, 1998.

These authors point out that health is more than freedom from illness or disease, and healing is more than curing a physical ailment. These Canadians draw their illustrations and experience as members of several congregations. They illustrate what it means to be a healing church. There is a review of the biblical basis for Christian healing, an emphasis on the wisdom of the body, an awareness of the shadow side of healing, and suggestions for ways of involving the community of faith, both laity and clergy. They seek to have the Spirit lead them in conducting their various forms of a healing ministry. There is a discussion of healing services, training members for the healing team, some of whom visit in homes as well as serving at healing stations in a church service. They discuss the need to have good boundaries and look after yourself as a healer. Too often the healer thinks of him/herself as primarily a giver and not also a receiver. This volume is loaded with spiritual wisdom and practical advice for the conduct of a multifaceted healing ministry in a local church.

Kelsey, Morton T., *Psychology, Medicine & Christian Healing.* San Francisco: Harper & Row, 1988. (Also published as *Healing and Christianity.*)

This comprehensive volume comes out of Kelsey's own experience in healing as an Episcopal parish priest (Agnes Sanford was a member of his congregation), studying the literature as a professor/scholar and author in the field of spirituality. Kelsey provides a fine survey of religious healing in the ancient world, a profound understanding of Jesus' healing ministry, the best available history of healing in the church over the past two thousand years, and a good treatment of the healing of emotions and their influence on the body. All of these are filtered through his great wisdom, which is influenced by a Jungian perspective. This work is meaty and takes patient reading. It is a wide-ranging historical, biblical, psychological, and theological study of healing and its place in the church today.

LeShan, Lawrence, *The Medium, the Mystic, and the Physicist.* New York: Viking, 1974.

LeShan provides the theoretical foundation for the imagery prayer that I use in contemplative healing training. LeShan studied the methods of healers from the United States England, and India. He then brought many healing techniques together into a single system in a five-day residential seminar that he taught all over the United

States, using spiritual exercises from many faith traditions as ways of opening to the numinous. Chapter 7 focuses on healing where he quotes Agnes Sanford: "Only love can generate the healing fire … when we pray in accordance with the will of God." LeShan was my mentor in healing and adviser for my doctoral dissertation. This book greatly expanded my worldview, and for me it is a classic.

———. *How to Meditate.* New York: Bantam, 1974 (paperback by arrangement with Little, Brown).

LeShan taught meditation exercises to hundreds of students, a dozen at a time, in his five-day healing seminars in the 1970s and '80s. In answer to the question "Why do we meditate?" he replies, "It's like coming home." LeShan suggests that "We meditate to find, to recover, to come back to something of ourselves we once dimly and unknowingly had and to reality, or to more of our capacity for love and zest and enthusiasm, or our knowledge that we are a part of the universe and can never be alienated or separated from it, or our ability to see and function in reality more effectively." LeShan once told me there was a "demand" inside of him to write this book that he could not ignore. He could not write or think about anything else during the three weeks that it took him to get it down on paper. This volume is good preparation or review for those who want to practice the imagery prayer in *Contemplative Healing* that is based on LeShan's healing method.

Lewis, Thomas, MD, Fari Amini, MD, and Richard Lannon, MD, *A General Theory of Love.* New York: Vintage Books, 2000.

"From birth to death, love is not just the focus of human experience but also the life force of the mind, determining our moods, stabilizing our bodily rhythms, and changing the structures of our brains. … Love makes us who we are, and who we can become." This is a revolutionary book in the field of psychotherapy and medicine that describes the limbic brain as the locus of emotional communication between mother and infant. This author is persuaded that God's healing force is communicated from one person to another through the nonlocal mechanism of *limbic resonance,* whether by laying on of hands or at a distance. He is also persuaded that this limbic connection is the vehicle that carries healing prayer. Love is the bottom line of all healing. This study of the evolutionary development of love from mother (and father), and later to others as the infant grows to adulthood is breaking much needed new ground, helping us to find a deeper understanding of what love is all about.

MacNutt, Francis, *Healing* .Altamont Springs, FL, Strang Communications, rev. ed., 1988.
———. *The Power to Heal.* New York: Bantam Books, 1979.

These books by a former Catholic priest came out of his rich experience in ministries of healing within the church. Early on he was influenced by the work of Agnes Sanford and other Protestant healers. These books draw on his extensive practical experience, psychological insight, a deep compassion, and a profound confidence in God's healing power. These books illustrate that there are many varieties of healing in the church.

Mehl-Madrona, Lewis, MD, *Coyote Medicine: Lessons from Native American Healing.* New York: Fireside Book, Simon & Schuster, 1997.

This is the story of a young physician's spiritual journey. He is half Cherokee, half Anglo, and a graduate of Stanford Medical School. He grew up with the belief system of our culture: materialism is the only reality. After medical school he became more aware of the world of spirit that interpenetrates matter and is just as real. Dr. Mehl-Madrona is a healer who draws on resources of spirit in this remarkable story, which well might be called "A Study in Intercessory Prayer." After graduating from medical school, he began studying Native American medicine, finding ways to integrate the material bio-medicine of our culture with the spiritual medicine practiced on this land hundreds of years before the white man came. He is a spiritual visionary and a wounded healer whose personal struggles along the way inspire and serve to authenticate his integration of technological and Native American medicine. His healing methods function as a unique bridge between heaven and earth. His spiritual journey is also a path of healing that has inspired, strengthened, and deepened this author's own journey.

Norberg, Tilda, and Robert D. Webber, *Stretch Out Your Hand.* Nashville, TN: Upper Room Books, revised 1998.

Norberg is a psychotherapist and United Methodist minister, and Webber is professor of New Testament at Lancaster Theological Seminary in Pennsylvania. In our culture any study of healing through prayer raises as many questions as it answers. Why isn't everyone healed? What is the role of faith? Is it fair to offer healing prayer and raise the hopes of an ill person that might later be dashed if he or she is not healed? The authors address these questions and many like them. This is an excellent introduction to healing for people in mainline churches who have never considered the subject, and it contains many personal accounts of healing. The book makes a fine six-week text for a study group. It deals with all the tough questions, is psychologically sophisticated, and is one of the few books on healing that sees a relationship between the healing of an individual and healing the wounds of a city or nation. It clearly describes the potential of a congregation to become a healing community.

Schlitz, Marilyn, and Tina Amorok with Marc S. Micozzi, eds., *Consciousness and Healing: Integral Approaches to Mind-Body Medicine,* St. Louis: Elsevier Churchill Livingstone, 2005.

In her preface, Marilyn Schlitz writes, "Since the rise of modern science, Western culture has assumed a separation between consciousness and matter, between mind and body, between humans and nature, between spirituality and science. These dualisms, deeply troublesome for science and philosophy, were also incorporated into the historical development of Western medicine." She observes that

"As they are commonly concerned, religion and science are indeed incompatible. But if properly understood and properly enlarged, these two realms may be incorporated within a framework that is at once true to their distinctions and yet comprehensive of both." This kind of inclusiveness is the subject of this book. Integral medicine demonstrates a willingness to bring together and view together our physiological, emotional, cognitive, social, ecological, and spiritual processes. Integral medicine also shows a willingness to formulate comprehensive theories that ask crucial questions about the relationship between consciousness and the physical world. Intercessory prayer for healing requires a focused state of consciousness to function. These authors have drawn together forty-six essays written by cutting-edge researchers and thinkers in a variety of fields who integrate and explain spiritual processes with their understanding of how mind, body, and spirit work together for wholeness and healing. Here are a few samples of these essays:

Dean Ornish, "Opening Your Heart: Anatomically, Emotionally, and Spiritually."

Larry Dossey, "The Return of Prayer."

Candace B. Pert, Henry E. Dreher, and Michael R. Ruff; "The Psychosomatic Network: Foundations of Mind-Body Medicine."

Roger Walsh, "The Practice of Essential Spirituality."

Stanley Krippner; "The Technologies of Shamanic States of Consciousness."

Jon Kabat-Zinn, "The Contemplative Mind in Society."

Nancy C. Maryboy and David H. Begay; "Restoration of Dynamic Balance: Traditional Ways of Healing Expressed Through Navajo Consciousness."

Sogyal Rinpoche, "The Spiritual Heart of Tibetan Medicine: Its Contribution to the Modern World."

Rachel Naomi Remen, "Recapturing the Soul of Medicine."

Brian Swimme and Thomas Berry, "Healthy Earth-Healthy Human."

Targ, Russell, and Jane Katra, *Miracles of Mind.* Novato, CA: New World Library, 1998.

Russell Targ is a physicist and author who was a pioneer in the development of the laser. Jane Katra has been a spiritual healer for more than twenty-five years. They examine how the mind's ability to transcend the limits of space and time is linked to our capacity for healing. The authors' collaboration began when Dr. Katra helped Targ cure himself of what was diagnosed as metastatic cancer. From this beginning the authors weave together compelling scientific evidence, ancient spiritual teachings, and dramatic personal stories—from witnessing folk healers in the Philippines to performing telepathic experiments between Moscow and San Francisco—to explore the potential of nonlocal mind. Incorporating Eastern spirituality and modern science, Targ and Katra explain how methods of alternative healing such as Therapeutic Touch or Qi Gong make use of the nonlocal concept of mind. The authors combine the perspectives of the physicist and the mystic to reveal the possibilities for mind-to-mind connections in a community of spirit.

Thomas, Leo, O. P., with Jan Alkire, *Healing Ministry—A Practical Guide.* Kansas City, MO: Sheed and Ward, 1994.

Father Thomas suggests that healing ministry belongs to the category of worship: its goal is to bring hurting people into an experience of God, meeting them in their need. This book is a primer that shows how to create a healing ministry that includes laity as well as clergy, and is a part of the overall ministry of pastoral care. This ministry includes pastoral visitation to the sick, grief ministry, Eucharistic ministers who bring communion to home-bound parishioners, and prayer groups that want to develop a sound ministry of healing. The authors outline the value of a healing team. This is a practical guide based on their thirty years of teaching laity and clergy, Protestant and Catholic, about healing prayer.

"Special Issue on Healing Prayer" *Alternative Therapies in Health and Medicine,* Vol. 3, No. 6, November 1997. A peer-reviewed journal edited by Larry Dossey, MD. This issue explores the role of prayer in healing. For a copy write Inno Vision Communications, AACN, 101 Columbia, Aliso Viejo, CA 92656. Phone (800) 899-1712. Single issue, $10.00.

EXPLORE: The Journal of Science and Healing is an interdisciplinary journal that addresses the scientific principles behind, and applications of, evidence-based healing practices from a wide variety of sources, including conventional, alternative, and cross-cultural medicine. Executive editor Larry Dossey, MD
Web site: www.explorejournal.com.

The organizations listed below focus part of their research on healing. I have been a member of both for some years, and find their conferences and publications very helpful and illuminating.

Institute of Noetic Sciences, 101 San Antonio Rd., Petaluma, CA 94952 (707) 775-3500; www.noetic.org

International Society for the Study of Subtle Energy and Energy Medicine
2770 Arapahoe Rd., Lafayette, CO 80026; (303) 425-4625; www.issseem.org

Author Bio

Francis Geddes, DMin, a United Church of Christ parish minister, has taught contemplative healing to more than nine hundred people in thirty congregations over three decades. His doctoral dissertation is titled "Healing Training in the Church." Geddes and wife Virginia live in Santa Rosa, California, where he offers healing at the Episcopal Church of the Incarnation.